Locomotive Traction

2020

PIP DUNN

abc
Crécy

Crécy.co.uk

Crécy

First published by Crécy Publishing Limited
2019

A CIP record for this book is available from the British Library

ISBN 9781910809631

Printed in the UK by Short Run Press

abc is an imprint of
Crécy Publishing Limited
1a Ringway Trading Estate
Shadowmoss Road
Manchester M22 5LH

www.crecy.co.uk

Front cover top: DB Cargo's 67010 drags LNER's 91125 on 1E06, the 0648 Glasgow Central-Kings Cross, past the Metro Centre on the Carlisle-Newcastle line on 29 September 2018. *Anthony Hicks*

Front cover bottom: GB Railfreight 60095 works 6N20, the 1754 Drax-Tyne, past Sherburn-in-Elmet on 24 May 2019. *Anthony Hicks*

Rear cover main: No. 40106 Atlantic Conveyor leaves Arley with the 1259 Kidderminster-Bridgnorth on 16 May 2019. *Glen Batten*

Rear below from left:
Colas has 17 Class 70s in its fleet. One of the second batch of seven locos, 70813 passes Glass's Crossing at Bathampton with 6C37, 1628 Westbury-Aberthaw empty cement tanks on 1 September 2017. *Glen Batten*

Preserved 31163 has been renumbered 97205 and repainted into the Research livery of the RailwayTechnical Centre once carried by 97204. On 4 May 2018, the loco was a visitor to the Keighley and Worth Valley Railway gala. *Stuart West*

On 7 April, 47813 Jack Frost and 47815 Lost Boys 68-88 pass Ashwell moving a rake of redundant ex-GWR HST trailers from Plymouth for store at Ely. *Bill Atkinson*

CONTENTS

Introduction

Welcome to the third edition of Crécy's Locomotive Traction book. This book lists all the diesel and electric locos that have run on the UK's National rail network, either in the past under British Rail or currently through train operating companies. By listing everything, even if the vehicle is no longer with us, you can still 'tick it off' or underline it should you so desire.

There are a lot of grey areas in how we classify a loco's status and often the lines are blurred. However, I have tried as best as I can to draw up distinct areas and therefore this book is split into four sections. They are:

Section 1 lists all the diesel and electric locomotives that are registered to run on the National Network Rail system, as well as those locos that are in store or withdrawn but owned or operated by franchised or Open Access Train Operating Companies. Even here there are some anomalies, mainly on shunting locos that may, or may not, be allowed out of the confines of the depots or yards at which they work. Locos owned by spot hire companies and third parties but used by franchised TOCs/FOCs are listed here.

Resplendent in Pullman livery, 67021, with 67024 on the rear, works 1Z60, the 1420 Sleaford-King's Cross private VSOE charter, approaching Wilsford on 17 April 2019. *Bill Atkinson*

These locos will have details of the key detail differences that affect the work they can undertake. Also listed is their TOPS Sector code as of 17 October 2019, their livery, owner and name if appropriate. Old numbers – pre-1973 D/E numbers and all previous TOPS numbers – are also listed.

Locos owned by preservation groups that are main line registered are listed in this section. Some locos may – presently – not be fully main line compliant (such as missing GSM-R) or being a shunting locomotive without TPWS but if they are used by a TOC then they are listed in this section. Not all locos in section 1 and 2 are on TOPS and have a pool code.

Section 2 lists all locos that are owned by spot hire companies but not main line registered or not on hire to FOCs/TOCs. These may be in industrial use or have been redeployed/sold for use abroad, and again relevant details are included. While these locos do not have current full main line registration, that could change.

Also included in this section are locos that have restricted NR registration – such as 25278, which can run between Middlesbrough and Whitby only.

It also details all ex-BR and ex-TOC/FOC locomotives that have been sold for private use or pending disposal. Also included in this section are any locos that have been sold to scrap merchants but have not yet been broken up, as they could be sold on for reuse.

Those locos moved abroad by the likes of DB Cargo or Freightliner, or sold for use by European operators, are also included here.

Section 3 details all locos classed as 'preserved', regardless of whether they have been restored or not. This includes locos that may never have run, or realistically are unlikely to ever run again. It does *not* include locos located at heritage sites that are owned by FOCs or spot hire companies; these are listed in section 2.

Finally, **section 4** lists all ex-BR locos that have been disposed of – and so no longer physically exist. These are listed in class order with their final number, and all previous numbers are also listed. However, their names are not included, nor are their detail difference and their disposal details.

Three-character owner and livery codes, sector codes and depot allocations are all listed in the appendices. Standard TOPS pool codes are used, but two-digit codes for depots and other locations are also listed.

Locos can, and of course will, change owner or status and so their inclusion in a certain section may change as events overtake them.

As always, the information in this book is in good faith and, as far as is known, correct to 17 October 2019. Any corrections, input to comments should be sent to the author via the publisher.

Pip Dunn, Spalding, October 2019

Codes for key loco detail differences

Codes for key loco detail differences

The key differences that affect the work or area that a loco can undertake are detailed. These are given by codes:

a   Train air brakes only
b   Operational steam heat boiler fitted
c   Tripcocks fitted
d   Dellner coupler fitted
e   Operational Electric Train Supply
f   Fire suppressant equipment fitted
g   ERTMS equipment fitted
h   Lickey banker auto coupler fitted
i   Non-operational steam heat boiler retained
j   Buffers fitted – where non standard
l   Scharfenberg coupler fitted
k   Engine stop-start equipment fitted
m   Multiple Working equipment fitted – where non standard
n   Multiple Working equipment removed – where non standard
o   No train heating capability
p   Snowplough brackets fitted (* main line loco fitted with snowploughs)
q   Remote monitoring equipment fitted
r   In-cab Radio Electronic Token Block (RETB) signalling fitted
s   Slow speed control fitted
t   Additional fuel tanks fitted
u   Push-pull fitted
v   Vacuum train brakes only
w   Waist level duplicate brake pipes fitted
x   Dual train brakes
y   Non-operational Electric Train Supply
z   Through Electric Train Supply wiring (loco is 'no heat')

All locos in sections 1 and 2 are deemed to be operational unless stated. All fittings relate to the loco at the time of press.

(S) Loco is in store in a serviceable condition. The loco may not have run for some time but could be returned to traffic relatively quickly. It may be stored pending an upgrade to meet group standards or may have been stopped to temporarily donate parts to another vehicle.

(U) Loco is in store in an unserviceable condition; the loco has been damaged, stripped, or laid up for a long period and would require major expenditure to return it to traffic. It may currently not meet group standards. Some of these locos may be for sale.

For preserved locos they are either classed as either operational (OP), actively under restoration (UR) or stored for parts donation, disposal or restoration to start at a later date (SU). Locos on static display are also listed as SU. D5910 is classed as UC – under construction.

Key abbreviations

AC   Alternating current

DC   Direct current

ETH   Electric Train Heat

ETS   Electric Train Supply

ft   foot

gal   gallon

GSM-R   Global System for Mobile Communications – Railway

hp   Horsepower

in   inch

kN   Kilonewton

kV   kilovolt

kW   kilowatt

km/h   kilometres per hour

lbf   pounds force

lit   litre

m   metre

mph   miles per hour

OTMR   On Train Monitoring and Recording ('black box')

TPWS   Train Protection and Warning System

V   Volt

No. 90019 *Multimodal* works 1B88, the 1606 King's Cross-Newark North Gate past Broad Fen Lane, Claypole, on 6 June 2019. DB Cargo Class 90s are no longer hired by LNER. *Bill Atkinson*

1 The main line fleet

Locos are listed by the current TOPS numbers, their previous numbers – including pre-TOPS D numbers, fittings, the sector to which the loco is allocated, the owner, livery, depot allocation or location the loco is at, and its current name.

Locos that had 89xxx numbers do NOT have these listed as they are not usually displayed other than in the cabs.

Class 08

Part of the mass order for the Standard BR 0-6-0 diesel electric shunter, of which over 1,000 were built from 1952, just a handful survive with a few train operators. More locos are owned by spot hire companies and listed in section 2.

Built by:	BR Derby, Crewe, Darlington, Horwich
Years introduced:	1952-62
Wheel arrangement:	0-6-0
Weight:	49-50 tons
Length:	29ft 3in (8.91m)
Engine Type:	English Electric 6KT
Engine output:	400hp (298kW)
Power at rail:	260hp (194kW)
Tractive effort:	35,000lbf (156kN)
Continuous tractive effort	11,100lbf (49kN)
Maximum design speed:	15-20mph (25-33km/h)
Brake Force:	19 tonnes
Route Availability:	5
Main generator type:	EE801-8E or E801-14E
Auxiliary generator type:	EE736-2D, EE736-4E or EE906-3D
Traction Motor type:	EE506-6A or EE506-7C
Fuel tank capacity:	668gal (3,036lit)
Multiple working type:	not fitted

Loco's current TOPS number	Previous official numbers carried	Key detail differences	Current TOPS Sector	Vehicle Owner	Current Livery	Current depot allocation or location	Current name (as displayed on the loco) Minor wording on crests, plaques or graphics is excluded
08410	D3525	ao	EFSH	GWR	GWR	PZ	
08411	D3526	ao	MBDL	RSS	BRW	WI (U)	
08417	D3532	ao	QADD	NET	NRY	DF (U)	
08418	D3533	ao	AWCA	WCR	EWS	CS	
08451	D3566	ao	ATZZ	ALS	BRW	LO	*MA SMITH*
08454	D3569	aod	ATLO	ALS	BRW	WD	
08472	D3587	ao	RFSH	WAB	BLK	EC	
08480	D3595	ao	MBDL	RSS	RSS	NC	
08483	D3598	ao	EFSH	GWR	BLK	LA	
08485	D3600	ao	AWCA	WCR	BRW	CS	
08507	D3662	ao	RTSO	RIV	OXB	ZG	
08511	D3673	ao	MBDL	RSS	RSS	ZG	
08523	D3685	ao	MRSO	RMS	RMS	WO	
08525	D3687	ao	EMSL	EMT	EMB	NL	*DUNCAN BEDFORD*
08530	D3692	ao	DDIN	POR	FLR	LH	
08531	D3693	ao	DDIN	POR	FPH	FX	
08571	D3738	ao	HBSH	WAB	BLK	DD	
08575	D3742	xo	DHLT	POR	FLR	LH (U)	

08585	D3752	ao	DDIN	POR	FLR	SM	*Vicky*
08588	D3755	ao	MRSO	RMS	RMS	DF	
08596	D3763	ao	HBSH	WAB	BLK	EC	
08611	D3778	ao	ATLO	ALS	BRW	WB	
08616	D3783	xo	EJLO	LON	LON	TS	*TYSELEY 100*
08617	D3784	aod	ATLO	ALS	BRW	OX	*Steve Purser*
08624	D3791	xo	DDIN	POR	FPH	FX	*Rambo Paul Ramsey*
08631	D3798	xo	MBDL	LSL	BRW	WO	
08641	D3808	ao	EFSH	GWR	BRW	LA	*Pride of Laira*
08644	D3811	ao	EFSH	GWR	BRW	LA	*Laira Diesel Depot 50 Years 1962-2012*
08645	D3812	ao	EFSH	GWR	KER	PZ	*St Piran*
08648	D3815	ao	MRSO	RMS	RMB	IS	
08670	D3837	ao	MBDL	RSS	RSS	BS	
08678	D3845	ao	AWCX	WCR	WCR	CS	
08683	D3850	ao	MBDL	RSS	EWS	NC	
08690	D3857	ao	EMSL	EMT	EMB	NL (U)	*DAVID THIRKILL*
08691	D3858	xo	DDIN	FLI	FLG	LH	*Terri*
08696	D3863	ao	ATLO	ALS	BRW	WB	
08704	D3871	ao	RTSO	LSL	OXB	EVR	
08721	D3889	ao	ATLO	ALS	BRW	WD	*Longsight TMD*
08735	D3903	ao	WQDA	ARV	ARV	EH	
08737	D3905	ao		LSL	EWS	SO	
08738	D3906	ao	MBDL	RSS	RSS	EH	
08754	D3922	ao	RMSX	RMS	RMS	IS	
08764	D3932	aod	ATZZ	RMS	BRW	PO	
08780	D3948	xo	LSLO	LSL	BLE	SO	
08785	D3953	ao	DDIN	POR	FLR	TP	
08790	D3958	ao	ATLO	ALS	BRW	EG	
08805	D3973	xo	EJLO	LON	RSR	SI	*Robin Jones 40 YEARS SERVICE*
08810	D3978	ao	MBDL	ARV	LNW	EH	*RICHARD J. WENHAM EASTLEIGH DEPOT*

Class 08s, once the most numerous locos in the BR fleet, are few and far between these days. On 28 April 2018, 08523 rests between shunting duties at Inverness. This loco is owned by RMS Locotec and has since moved to the Weardale Railway. *Graeme Elgar*

08818	D3986	ao	HNRL	HNR	GBR	FG		*MOLLY*
08822	D3990	ao	EFSH	GWR	ICS	PM		*Dave Mills*
08834	D4002	xo	HNRL	HNR	HNR	AN		
08836	D4004	ao	EFSH	GWR	GWR	RG		
08868	D4036	xo	MBDL	ARV	LNW	CP		
08887	D4117	ao	ATZZ	ALS	BRW	PO		
08891	D4121	ao	DHLT	POR	FLR	ZG (U)		
08899	D4129	xo	EMSL	EMT	MID	DY		*Midland Counties Railway 175 Years 1839-2014*
08908	D4138	ao	EMSL	EMT	EMB	NL		*IVAN STEPHENSON*
08925	D4155	ao	GBWM	GBR	GWS	WG		
08934	D4164	ao	GBWM	GBR	GWS	BH (U)		
08948	D4178	aol	GPSS	EUK	EUK	TI		
08950	D4180	ao	EMSL	EMT	EMB	NL		*DAVID LIGHTFOOT*
08954	D4184	ao	HNRL	HNR	BRW	PO		

Note: 08451/795 have buckeye couplers

Note: 08735 has a swinghead coupler and remote control equipment

Note: Not all Class 08/09s are passed to run on the main line and may be restricted to designated areas. TOCs that hire shunting locomotives may have these vehicles swapped occasionally with those listed in section 2.

Class 09

Another version of the BR standard shunter the Class 09s had a higher top speed. Twenty-six were originally built, but 12 were later converted by BR from Class 08s.

Built by:	BR Darlington, Horwich
Years introduced:	1959-62
Wheel arrangement:	0-6-0
Weight:	49 tons
Length:	29ft 3in (8.91m)
Engine Type:	English Electric 6KT
Engine output:	400hp (298kW)
Power at rail:	260hp (194kW)
Tractive effort:	25,000lbf (111kN)
Continuous tractive effort	8,800lbf (39kN)
Maximum design speed:	27mph (34km/h)
Brake Force:	19 tonnes
Route Availability:	5
Main generator type:	EE801-8E or E801-14E
Auxiliary generator type:	EE906-3D
Traction Motor type:	EE506-10C
Fuel tank capacity:	668gal (3,036lit)
Multiple Working type:	Not fitted

09002	D3666	ao	GBWM	GBR	GWS	WG	
09007	D3671	aow		LOL	GWS	WN	
09009	D3720	ao	GBWM	GBR	GWS	DL	

Class 20

An initial 20 English Electric Type 1s were part of the 1955 Pilot Scheme leading to a further 208 being built in 1957-68. A handful remain in use on the main line use. The eight GBEE locos – owned by HNRC – have ended their hire contract with GBRf and are available for spot hire use. The MOLO locos are used for occasional spot hire work.

Built by:	English Electric Vulcan Foundry or Robert Stephenson & Hawthorns
Years introduced:	1957-68
Wheel arrangement:	Bo-Bo
Weight:	73 tons
Length:	46ft 9in (14.26m)
Engine Type:	English Electric 8SVT Mk 2
Engine output:	1,000hp (746kW)
Power at rail:	770hp (574kW)
Tractive effort:	42,000lbf (187kN)
Continuous tractive effort	25,000lbf (111kN)
Maximum design speed:	75mph (120km/h)
Brake Force:	35 tons
Route Availability:	5
Main generator type:	EE819-3C
Auxiliary generator type:	EE911-2B
Traction Motor type:	EE526/5D (20007), 526/8D (others)
Fuel tank capacity:	380gal (1,727lit)
Multiple Working type:	Blue Star

Class 20/0 – standard locos

20007	D8007	ao	MOLO	MOW	GYP	SK	
20096	D8096	aocp	GBEE	HNR	BRB	BH	*Ian Goddard 1938-2016*
20107	D8107	aocp	GBEE	HNR	BRB	BH	
20118	D8118	aop	GBEE	HNR	RSR	BH	*Saltburn-by-the-Sea*
20132	D8132	aop	GBEE	HNR	RSR	BH	*Barrow Hill Depot*
20142	D8142	xocp	MOLO	MOW	MRM	SK	*SIR JOHN BETJEMAN*
20189	D8189	xop	MOLO	MOW	BRB	SK	
20205	D8305	aop	MOLO	MOW	BRB	SK	
20227	D8327	xop	MOLO	CTL	MRM	SK	*SHERLOCK HOLMES*

Note: 20227 is on long term hire to the North Norfolk Railway

Class 20/3 – refurbished locos

Details as per Class 20/0

Route Availability:	5 (20301-305), 6 – 20308-314
Traction Motor type:	EE526/5D (20301/312), 526/8D (others)
Fuel tank capacity:	640gal (2,909lit, 20301-305), 1,090gal (4,909lit, 20306-315),
Multiple Working type:	DRS system

20301	20047, D8047	aotp	XHSS	DRS	DRC	BH (U)	
20302	20084, D8084	aotp	XHSS	DRS	DRC	KM	
20303	20127, D8127	aotp	XHSS	DRS	DRC	KM	*Max Joule 1958-1999*
20304	20120, D8120	aotp	XHSS	DRS	DRC	BH (U)	
20305	20095, D8095	aotp	XHSS	DRS	DRC	KM	
20308	20187, D8187	aotp	XHSS	DRS	DRC	BH (U)	
20309	20075, D8075	aotp	XHSS	DRS	DRC	BH (U)	
20311	20102, D8102	aotcp	XHCK	HNR	HNO	BH	
20312	20042, D8042	aotp	XHSS	DRS	DRC	BH (U)	
20314	20117, D8117	aotcp	XHCK	HNR	HNO	BH	

Note: 20302/303/305 were reinstated for RHTT operation from York for autumn 2019, and then should return to store pending developments on their future requirements on these trains.

Class 20/9 – former Hunslet Barclay locos
Details as per Class 20/0
    Traction Motor type: 526/8D

20901	20101, D8101	aotcp	GBEE	HNR	GBR	WK
20905	20225, D8325	aotcp	GBEE	HNR	GBR	BH (S)

Class 31
A derivative of an initial 20-strong order for the 1955 Pilot Scheme, the fleet eventually totalled 263 locos. All were new with Mirrlees engines but these proved unreliable and all were replaced by EE engines in 1964-69. The pilot scheme locos were all withdrawn by 1980, and 70 locos were later converted to have ETH. Just 31128 is currently fit for use on the main line use.

Built by:	Brush Ltd, Loughborough
Years introduced:	1964-69 (converted from Class 30s)
Wheel arrangement:	A1A-A1A
Weight:	107-111 tons
Length:	56ft 9in (17.29m)
Engine Type:	English Electric 12SVT
Engine output:	1,470hp (1,097kW)
Power at rail:	1,170hp (872kW)
Tractive effort:	35,900lbf (160kN)
Continuous tractive effort	18,700lbf (83kN)
Maximum design speed:	90mph (144km/h)
Brake Force:	49 tons
Route Availability:	5
Main generator type:	Brush TG160-48
Auxiliary generator type:	Brush TG69-42
Traction Motor type:	Brush TM73-68
Fuel tank capacity:	530gal (2,385lit)
Multiple Working type:	Blue Star

Main Line Class 20s are in short supply, and following the end of duties with GB Railfreight, the eight HNRC locos are only used occasionally on short term spot hire work. On May 27 2019, 20096/107 pass Ancaster with a Swindon-Skegness railtour. *Anthony Hicks*

Currently the only Class 31 with full main line registration is Nemesis Rail's 31128 *Charybdis*, which is used by West Cost Railways. On 7 August 2019, it passes Barton-under-Needwood hauling 86259 *Les Ross* from Burton to Lichfield. *Ian Nightingale*

Class 31/1 – standard locos

31128	D5546	xop	NRLO	NEM	BRB	BU	*Charybdis*

Class 33

Type 3 design built by BRCW for the Southern Region, fitted with dual brakes and electric train heat from new. Nineteen locos were converted to push-pull operation (Class 33/1s) and the final 12 were built with a narrower body profile for working on the gauge-restricted Hastings line (Class 33/2). Three remain in use with WCR, while D6515 is a preserved loco but with full main line registration that is used occasionally by WCR and GBRf.

Built by:	Birmingham RC&W
Years introduced:	1960-62
Wheel arrangement:	Bo-Bo
Weight:	77 tons
Length:	50ft 9in (15.47m)
Engine Type:	Sulzer 8LDA28A
Engine output:	1,550hp (1,154kW)
Power at rail:	1,215hp (906kW)
Tractive effort:	45,000lbf (200kN)
Continuous tractive effort	26,000lbf (116kN)
ETH generator type:	Crompton Parkinson CAG392-A1
ETH index:	48
Maximum design speed:	85mph (137km/h)

Brake Force:	35 tons
Route Availability:	6
Main generator type:	Crompton Parkinson CAG391-B1
Auxiliary generator type:	Crompton Parkinson CAG193-A1
Traction Motor type:	Crompton Parkinson C171-C2
Fuel tank capacity:	750gal (3,410lit)
Multiple Working type:	Blue Star

Class 33/0 – standard locos

33012	D6515	xep*	MBDL	SOA	GYP	SR	*Lt Jenny Lewis RN*
33025	D6543	xyp*	AWCA	WCR	WCR	CS	
33029	D6547	aop*	AWCA	WCR	WCR	CS	
33030	D6548	ayp	AWCX	WCR	DRU	CS (U)	

Class 33/2 – narrow 'Hastings gauge' body

| 33207 | D6592 | aop* | AWCA | WCR | WCR | CS | *Jim Martin* |

There are just four main line certified Class 33s: privately owned D6515 *Lt Jenny Lewis RN* and three WCR locos. The former leads WCR's 33029 as they pass Wyke Champflower, near Castle Cary, with 1Z34, the 1440 Weymouth-Crewe charter on 23 March 2019. *Mark Pike*

Class 37

Standard Diesel Electric Type 3 design, of which 309 were built. A total of 135 locos were refurbished in the late 1980s, including 31 with ETH (Class 37/4), 44 with added ballast weights (Class 37/7) and six with test bed alternative engines (Class 37/9). Twelve locos were later converted with through ETH wiring for Eurostar. They remain in use with DRS, WCR, LSL, Colas Rail and ROG.

Built by:	English Electric, Vulcan Foundry or Robert Stephenson & Hawthorns
Years introduced:	1960-65
Wheel arrangement:	Co-Co
Weight:	102-108 tons
Length:	61ft 6in (18.74m)
Engine Type:	English Electric 12CSVT
Engine output:	1,750hp (1,304kW)
Power at rail:	1,250hp (932kW)
Tractive effort:	55,500lbf (247kN)
Continuous tractive effort	35,000lbf (156kN)
Maximum design speed:	90mph (144km/h)
Brake Force:	50 tons
Route Availability:	5
Main generator type:	EE822-10G, EE822-13G or EE822-16J
Auxiliary generator type:	EE911/5C
Traction Motor type:	EE538-1A or EE538-5A
Fuel tank capacity:	890gal (4,046lit) or t – 1,690gal (7,682lit)
Multiple Working type:	Blue Star (DRS system: 37038/059/069/218/259)

Class 37/0 – standard locos

37025	D6725	xbprz*	COTS	STG	BLL	BT	Inverness TMD
37038	D6738	aot	XHNC	DRS	DRN	KM	
37057	D6757	xi	COTS	COL	GYP	HQ	
37059	D6759	aotr	XHNC	DRS	DRN	KM	
37069	D6769	aotr	XHNC	DRS	DRN	KM	
37099	D6799, 37324	xirp*	COTS	COL	COL	RU	MERL EVANS 1947-2016
37116	D6816	xor	COTS	COL	COL	HQ	
37165	D6865, 37374	xot		WCR	CCT	CS (U)	
37175	D6875	xorp*	COTS	COL	COL	HQ	
37190	D6890, 37314	xip*	MBDL	LSL	BRB	CD (U)	
37218	D6918	aotrp*	XHNC	DRS	DRN	KM	
37219	D6919	aotrp*	COTS	COL	COL	HQ	Jonty Jarvis 8-12-1998 to 18-3-2005
37254	D6954	aotrp	COTS	COL	COL	HQ	Cardiff Canton
37259	D6959, 37380	aotrp	XHNC	DRS	DRC	KM	

Note: 37219 has monitoring equipment mounting brackets fitted at No. 2 end

Class 37/4 – refurbished locos with ETH

Details as per 37/0 except:

Converted by:	BREL Crewe
Years introduced:	1985/86
Tractive effort:	57,440lbf (256kN)
Continuous tractive effort	41,250lbf (184kN)
ETH alternator type:	Brush BAH701
ETH index:	30
Design speed:	80mph (128km/h)
Main alternator type:	Brush BA1005A
Auxiliary alternator type:	Brush BA606A
Multiple Working type:	Blue Star (DRS system and Blue Star: 37423)

37401	D6968, 37268	aetp*	XHAC	DRS	BLL	KM	Mary Queen of Scots
37402	D6974, 37274	aetp*	XHAC	DRS	BLL	KM	Stephen Middlemore 23.12.1954 – 8.6.2013
37403	D6607, 37307	xetfp*	XHAC	SRP	BLL	KM	Isle of Mull
37405	D6982, 37282	aerftp*	XHAC	DRS	DRC	KM	
37407	D6605, 37305	aetfp*	XHAC	DRS	BLL	KM	Blackpool Tower
37409	D6970, 37270	aetfp*	XHAC	DRS	BLL	KM	Lord Hinton
37418	D6971, 37271	xetp*	COTS	BEN	BLL	HQ	
37419	D6991, 37291	aerftp*	XHAC	DRS	ICM	KM	Carl Haviland 1954-2012
37421	D6967, 37267	aetfp*	COTS	COL	COL	HQ	
37422	D6966, 37266	aerftp	XHSS	DRS	DRU	GB (U)	
37423	D6996, 37296	aerftp*	XHAC	DRS	DRX	KM	Spirit of the Lakes
37424	D6979, 37279	aetfp*	XHAC	DRS	BLL	KM	Avro Vulcan XH558
37425	D6992, 37292	aerftp*	XHSS	DRS	DRC	DF (S)	Sir Robert McAlpine/Concrete Bob

Note: 37424 carries the numbers 37558 on its bodysides

Class 37/5 – refurbished locos with no heating

Details as per Class 37/4 except:

Years introduced:	1985-89
Tractive effort:	55,590lbf (248kN)
Multiple Working type:	Blue Star (DRS system and Blue Star: 37667)

37510	D6812, 37112	aotp	SROG	EPX	EPX	LR (S)	
37516	D6786, 37086	xotrp*	AWCA	WCR	WCR	CS	Loch Laidon
37517	D6718, 37018	xotp		WCR	LHO	CS (U)	
37518	D6776, 37076	xotrp*	AWCA	WCR	WCR	CS	
37521	D6817, 37117	xotp*	COTS	SW	COL	BH	

DRS's 37402 Stephen Middlemore works 5Z02, the 1613 Leeds-Derby empty inspection saloon past Holbeck on 18 July 2019. Anthony Hicks

Class 37/6 – refurbished former Eurostar locos

Details as per Class 37/5 except:

Years introduced:	1995-96
Design speed:	90mph (144km/h)
Multiple Working type:	Blue Star (DRS system: 37602/605-611, DRS system and Blue Star: 37601/603/604)

Originally modified with through ETH wiring

37601	D6705, 37005, 37501	aotdrp*	GROG	ROG	EPX	LR	*Perseus*
37602	D6782, 37082, 37502	aotrzp*	XHNC	DRS	DRC	ZG (S)	
37603	D6739, 37039, 37604	aotp	XHSS	DRS	DRC	LT (S)	
37604	D6707, 37007, 37506	aotp	XHSS	DRS	DRC	LT (S)	
37605	D6736, 37036, 37507	aotrp	XHSS	DRS	DRC	DF (U)	
37606	D6790, 37090, 37508	aotp*	XHNC	DRS	DRC	GB (S)	
37607	D6803, 37103, 37511	aotpr	COTS	COL	DRU	BH (S)	
37608	D6722, 37022, 37512	aotrp*	GROG	EPX	EPX	LR	*Andromeda*
37609	D6815, 37115, 37514	aotrp*	XHSS	DRS	DRC	LT (S)	
37610	D6881, 37181, 37687	aotrp	COTS	HNR	BLU	BH	
37611	D6871, 37171, 37690	aotdrp*	GROG	EPX	EPX	LR	*Pegasus*
37612	D6879, 37179, 37691	aotpr	COTS	HNR	DRU	BH	

Class 37/5 (continued)

37667	D6851, 37151	aotrp*	LSLO	LSL	GYP	CD	
37668	D6957, 37257	xotgrp	AWCA	WCR	WCR	CS	
37669	D6829, 37129	xotgrp	AWCA	WCR	WCR	CS	
37676	D6826, 37126	xotrp*	AWCA	WCR	WCR	CS	*Loch Rannoch*
37685	D6934, 37234	xotrp*	AWCA	WCR	WCR	CS	*Loch Arkaig*

Class 37/7 – refurbished locos with ballast weights

Details as per Class 37/5 except:

Years introduced:	1986-88
Weight:	120 tons
Tractive effort:	62,000lbf (276kN)
Brake Force:	60 tons
Route Availability:	7
Multiple Working type:	Blue Star (DRS system and Blue Star: 37716)

37706	D6716, 37016	xotrp*	AWCA	WCR	WCR	CS	
37710	D6744, 37044	xotp		WCR	LHO	CS (U)	
37712	D6802, 37102	xotp	AWCX	WCR	WCR	CS (U)	
37716	D6794, 37094	aotfp*	XHNC	DRS	DRN	KM	
37800	D6843, 37143	aotdp	GROG	EPX	EPX	LR	*Cassiopeia*
37884	D6883, 37183	aotp	GROG	EPX	EPX	LR	*Cepheus*

Note: 37884 has a tightlock coupler fitted

Class 37/9 – refurbished locos with trial engines

Details as per Class 37/7 except:

Years introduced:	1986
Engine Type:	37901-904 – Mirrlees MB275T
	37905-906 – Ruston RK270T
Engine output:	1,800hp (1,340kW) – 37901-906
Power at rail:	1,300hp (940kW) – 37901-906
Tractive effort	62,680lbf (279kN)
Multiple Working type:	Blue Star

37901	D6850, 37150	xotp	EPUK	EPX	EPX	LR (U)	*Mirrlees Pioneer*
37905	D6836, 37136	xotp	UKRM	UKR	GYP	LR (U)	
37906	D6906, 37206	xotp	UKRM	UKR	RFO	BAT (U)	

Class 97 – Network Rail Class 37/0s with ERTMS

Details as per Class 37/0 except:

Years introduced:	2008
Multiple Working type:	Blue Star

97301	D6800, 37100	xogp	QETS	NET	NRY	ZA	
97302	D6870, 37170	xogp*	QETS	NET	NRY	ZA	*Ffestiniog and Welsh Highland Railways/Eheilffrdd Ffestiniog Ac Eryri*
97303	D6878, 37178	xogp*	QETS	NET	NRY	ZA	
97304	D6917, 37217	xogp	QETS	NET	NRY	ZA	*John Tiley*

Colas Class 37s have been provided to Transport for Wales for some Cardiff-Rhymney turns. On 29 August, 37025 *Inverness TMD* – on long-term hire from the Scottish Class 37 Group – stands at the terminus. *Glen Batten*

Class 40

A pilot scheme of ten locos led to another 190 locos being ordered. All were withdrawn by 1985 bar the pioneer loco D200 (40122), which was retained for special duties until withdrawal in 1988. No. 40145 returned to the main line in 2002 and 40013 in 2018. Both are currently undergoing repairs.

Built by:	English Electric, Vulcan Foundry
Years introduced:	1958-62
Wheel arrangement:	1Co-Co1
Length:	69ft 6in (21.18m)
Weight:	136 tons
Engine Type:	English Electric 16SVT Mk 2
Engine output:	2,000hp (1,492kW)
Power at rail:	1,550hp (1,156kW)
Tractive effort:	52,000lb
Continuous tractive effort	30,900lbf (137kN)
Maximum design speed:	90mph (144km/h)
Brake Force:	51 tons
Route Availability:	6
Main generator type:	EE822
Auxiliary generator type:	EE911-2B
Traction Motor type:	EE 526-5D
Fuel tank capacity:	710gal (3,195lit)
Multiple Working type:	Blue Star

40013	D213	xo	LSLO	SW	GYP	CD	*ANDANIA*
40145	D345	xo	CFSL	CFP	BRB	BH (U)	

D213 *Andania* passes Slindon, between Stafford and Crewe, with a loaded test run on 8 August 2018. *Ian Nightingale*

Class 43

The HST power cars (not to be confused with the Class 43 North British Warship Diesel hydraulics), run in pairs, either end of a rake of Mk 3 trailer vehicles. All were built with Paxman Valenta engines but all were re-engined with either MTU or VP185 engines. Just three have been written off after collisions. The Virgin East Coast locos will be replaced by IET multiple units by early 2020. Fifty-four power cars have all been moved to Haymarket to work for ScotRail and most have now been repainted. Great Western Railway has ended its use of power cars on main express trains from London but retains several short sets for use on trains in the West Country. All these power cars will be named after Castles in 2020.

Built by:	BREL Crewe
Years introduced:	1976-82
Wheel arrangement:	Bo-Bo
Weight:	70 tons
Length:	58ft 5in (17.80m)
Original engine:	Paxman Valenta 12RP200L (all since removed)
Replacement engines:	Mirrlees Blackstone MB190 (all since removed)
	Paxman 12VP185 (EMPC locos only)
	MTU16V4000 R41R
Engine output:	2,700hp (2,010kW)
Power at rail:	1,770hp (1,320kW)
Tractive effort:	17,980lbf (80kN)
Continuous Tractive effort:	10,340lbf (46kN)
Maximum design speed:	125mph (200km/h)
Brake force:	35t
Route Availability:	6
Main alternator type:	Brush BA1001B (VP185 locos), Brush BA1001C (MTU locos)
Traction Motor type:	43002-123/153-198 (Brush TMH68-46), 43124-152 (GECG417AZ)
Fuel tank capacity:	1,030gal (4,680lit)
Multiple Working type:	Within class only

43003	ae	HAPC	ANG	SCT	HA	
43004	ae	EFPC	ANG	GWT	LA	
43005	ae	EFPC	ANG	GWT	LA	
43009	ae	EFPC	ANG	FGB	LA	
43010	ae	EFPC	ANG	FGB	LA	
43012	ae	HAPC	ANG	SCT	HA	
43013	aej	QCAR	POR	NRY	EC	*Mark Carne CBE*
43014	aej	QCAR	POR	NRY	EC	*The Railway Observer*
43015	ae	HAPC	ANG	SCT	HA	
43016	ae	EFPC	ANG	GWT	LA	
43017	ae	SCEL	ANG	FGB	ELY (S)	
43018	ae	SCEL	ANG	FGB	HA (S)	
43020	ae	EFPC	ANG	FGB	LA	*mtu Power Passion Partnership*
43021	ae	HAPC	ANG	SCT	HA	
43022	ae	EFPC	ANG	FGB	LA	*The Duke of Edinburgh's Award Diamond Jubilee*
43023	ae	EFPC	ANG	FGB	LA	*SQN LDR HAROLD STARR ONE OF THE FEW*
43024	ae	SCEL	ANG	FGB	ELY (S)	
43025	ae	SCEL	ANG	FGB	ELY (S)	
43026	ae	HAPC	ANG	SCT	HA	

43027	ae	EFPC	ANG	FGB	LA	
43028	ae	HAPC	ANG	SCT	HA	
43029	ae	EFPC	ANG	FGB	LA	
43030	ae	HAPC	ANG	SCT	HA	
43031	ae	HAPC	ANG	SCT	HA	
43032	ae	HAPC	ANG	SCT	HA	
43033	ae	HAPC	ANG	SCT	HA	
43034	ae	HAPC	ANG	SCT	HA	
43035	ae	HAPC	ANG	SCT	HA	
43036	ae	HAPC	ANG	SCT	HA	
43037	ae	HAPC	ANG	SCT	HA	
43040	ae	EFPC	ANG	GWT	LA	
43041	ae	EFPC	ANG	GWT	LE	*Meningitis Trust Support for Life*
43042	ae	EFPC	ANG	GWT	LE	
43043	ae	EMPC	POR	EMB	NL	
43044	ae	EMPC	POR	EMB	NL	
43045	ae	EMPC	POR	EMB	NL	
43046	ae	EMPC	POR	EMB	NL	
43047	ae	EMPC	POR	EMB	NL	
43048	ae	EMPC	POR	EMB	NL	*TCB Miller MBE*
43049	ae	EMPC	POR	EMB	NL	*Neville Hill*
43050	ae	EMPC	POR	EMA	NL	
43052	ae	EMPC	POR	EMB	NL	
43053	ae	SBXL	POR	FGB	LM (S)	
43054	ae	EMPC	POR	EMB	NL	
43055	ae	EMPC	POR	EMB	NL	*The Sheffield Star 125 Years*
43056	ae	SBXL	POR	FGB	LM (S)	
43058	ae	IECP	POR	EMB	NL	
43059	ae	EMPC	POR	EMB	NL	
43060	ae	EMPC	POR	EMB	NL	
43061	ae	IECP	POR	EMB	NL	*The Fearless Foxes*
43062	ae	QCAR	POR	NRY	EC	*John Armitt*
43063	ae	EFPC	POR	FGB	LE	
43064	ae	EMPC	POR	EMB	NL	
43066	ae	EMPC	POR	EMB	NL	
43069	ae	SBXL	POR	FGB	LM (S)	
43070	ae	SBXL	POR	FGB	LM (S)	
43071	ae	EFPC	POR	FGB	LE	
43073	ae	EMPC	POR	EMB	NL	
43075	ae	EMPC	POR	EMB	NL	
43076	ae	EMPC	POR	EMB	NL	*IN SUPPORT OF HELP FOR HEROES*
43078	ae	SBXL	POR	FGB	LM (S)	
43079	ae	SBXL	POR	FGB	LM (S)	
43081	ae	EMPC	POR	EMA	NL	
43082	ae	EMPC	POR	EMB	NL	*RAILWAY Children*
43083	ae	EMPC	POR	EMB	NL	
43086	ae	EFPC	POR	FGB	LE	
43087	ae	SBXL	POR	FGB	LM (S)	
43088	ae	EFPC	POR	FGB	LE	
43089	ae	EMPC	POR	EMB	NL	
43091	ae	SBXL	POR	FGB	LM (S)	
43092	ae	EFPC	FIR	GWT	LE	
43093	ae	EFPC	FIR	GWA	LE	*Old Oak Common HST Depot 1976-2018*
43094	ae	EFPC	FIR	GWT	LE	
43097	ae	EFPC	FIR	GWT	LE	*Environment Agency*

43098	ae	EFPC	FIR	GWT	LE	
43122	ae	EFPC	FIR	GWT	LE	
43124	ae	HAPC	ANG	SCT	HA	
43125	ae	HAPC	ANG	SCT	HA	
43126	ae	HAPC	ANG	SCT	HA	
43127	ae	HAPC	ANG	SCT	HA	
43128	ae	HAPC	ANG	SCT	HA	
43129	ae	HAPC	ANG	SCT	HA	
43130	ae	HAPC	ANG	SCT	HA	
43131	ae	HAPC	ANG	SCT	HA	
43132	ae	HAPC	ANG	SCT	HA	Aberdeen Station 150th Anniversary
43133	ae	HAPC	ANG	SCT	HA	
43134	ae	HAPC	ANG	SCT	HA	
43135	ae	HAPC	ANG	SCT	HA	
43136	ae	HAPC	ANG	SCT	HA	
43137	ae	HAPC	ANG	SCT	HA	
43138	ae	HAPC	ANG	SCT	HA	
43139	ae	HAPC	ANG	SCT	HA	
43140	ae	HAPC	ANG	SCT	HA	
43141	ae	HAPC	ANG	SCT	HA	
43142	ae	HAPC	ANG	FGB	HA	
43143	ae	HAPC	ANG	SCT	HA	
43144	ae	HAPC	ANG	FGB	HA	
43145	ae	HAPC	ANG	SCT	HA	
43146	ae	HAPC	ANG	SCT	HA	
43147	ae	HAPC	ANG	SCT	HA	
43148	ae	HAPC	ANG	SCT	HA	
43149	ae	HAPC	ANG	SCT	HA	
43150	ae	HAPC	ANG	SCT	HA	
43151	ae	HAPC	ANG	FGB	HA	
43152	ae	HAPC	ANG	SCT	HA	
43153	ae	EFPC	FIR	GWT	LA	
43154	ae	EFPC	FIR	FGB	LA	
43155	ae	EFPC	FIR	FGB	LA	The Red Arrows 50 Seasons of Excellence
43156	ae	EFPC	POR	FGB	LA	Dartington International Summer School
43158	ae	EFPC	FIR	FGB	LA	
43159	ae	SBXL	POR	FGB	LM (S)	
43160	ae	EFPC	POR	FGB	LA	Sir Moir Lockhead
43161	ae	EFPC	POR	FGB	LA	
43162	ae	EFPC	POR	FGB	LA	
43163	ae	HAPC	ANG	SCT	HA	
43164	ae	HAPC	ANG	SCT	HA	
43165	ae	SCEL	ANG	FGB	ELY (S)	
43168	ae	HAPC	ANG	SCT	HA	
43169	ae	HAPC	ANG	SCT	HA	
43170	ae	EFPC	ANG	GWT	LA	
43171	ae	EFPC	ANG	FGB	LA	
43172	ae	EFPC	ANG	HAR	LA	Harry Patch The last survivor of the trenches
43174	ae	SCEL	ANG	FGB	ELY (S)	
43175	ae	HAPC	ANG	SCT	HA	
43176	ae	HAPC	ANG	SCT	HA	
43177	ae	HAPC	ANG	SCT	HA	
43179	ae	HAPC	ANG	SCT	HA	
43180	ae	EFPC	POR	FGB	LA	
43181	ae	HAPC	ANG	SCT	HA	

43182		ae	HAPC	ANG	SCT	HA	
43183		ae	HAPC	ANG	SCT	HA	
43185		ae	SCEL	ANG	ICS	ELY (S)	
43186		ae	EFPC	ANG	GWT	LA	
43187		ae	EFPC	ANG	GWT	LA	
43188		ae	EFPC	ANG	GWT	LA	
43189		ae	EFPC	ANG	GWT	LA	
43190		ae	SCEL	ANG	FGB	ELY (S)	
43191		ae	EFPC	ANG	FGB	LA	
43192		ae	EFPC	ANG	GWT	LA	
43193		ae	SBXL	POR	FGB	LM (S)	
43194		ae	EFPC	FIR	GWT	LA	
43195		ae	EFPC	ANG	FGB	LA (U)	
43196		ae	EFPC	POR	FGB	LA	
43197		ae	SCEL	POR	FGB	LM (S)	
43198		ae	EFPC	FIR	GWT	LA	*Driver Stan Martin/Driver Brian Cooper*

Note: 43010/020/023/027 are on hire to Hull Trains

Note: the following locomotives are due to be named by GWR in 2019/20

43004 *Caerphilly Castle*
43005 *St. Michael's Mount*
43016 *Powderham Castle*
43040 *Berry Pomeroy Castle*
43041 *St. Catherine's Castle*
43042 *Tregenna Castle*
43092 *Cromwell's Castle*
43093 *Castle-an-Dinas*
43094 *St. Mawes Castle*
43097 *Castle Drogo*
43098 *Walton Castle*
43122 *Dunster Castle*
43153 *Chûn Castle*
43154 *Compton Castle*
43155 *Rougemont Castle*
43170 *Chepstow Castle*
43158 *Kingswear Castle*
43186 *Taunton Castle*
43187 *Cardiff Castle*
43188 *Newport Castle*
43189 *Launceston Castle*
43192 *Trematon Castle*
43194 *Okehampton Castle*

Class 43/2

Details as per 43/0 fitted with MTU engines

43206	43006	ae	IECP	ANG	VEC	EC	
43207	43007	ae	EHPC	ANG	XCT	EC	
43208	43008	ae	IECP	ANG	VEC	EC	*Lincolnshire Echo*
43238	43038	ae	IECP	ANG	NRA	EC	*National Railway Museum 40 Years 1975-2015*
43239	43039	ae	IECP	ANG	VEC	EC	
43251	43051	ae	IECP	POR	VEC	EC	
43257	43057	ae	IECP	POR	VEC	EC	*Bounds Green*
43272	43072	ae	IECP	POR	VEC	EC	
43274	43074	ae	IECP	POR	VEC	EC	*Spirit of Sunderland*

43277	43077	ae	IECP	POR	VEC	EC	
43285	43085	ae	EHPC	POR	XCT	EC	
43290	43090	ae	IECP	POR	VEC	EC	
43295	43095	ae	IECP	ANG	VEC	EC	
43296	43096	ae	IECP	ANG	VEC	EC	
43299	43099	ae	IECP	POR	VEC	EC	
43300	43100	ae	IECP	POR	VEC	EC	
43301	43101	ae	EHPC	POR	XCT	EC	
43302	43102	ae	IECP	POR	VEC	EC	
43303	43103	ae	EHPC	POR	XCT	EC	
43304	43104	ae	EHPC	ANG	XCT	EC	
43305	43105	ae	IECP	ANG	VEC	EC	
43306	43106	ae	IECP	ANG	VEC	EC	
43307	43107	ae	IECP	ANG	VEC	EC	
43308	43108	ae	IECP	ANG	VEC	EC	*HIGHLAND CHIEFTAIN*
43309	43109	ae	IECP	ANG	VEC	EC	
43310	43110	ae	IECP	ANG	VEC	EC	
43311	43111	ae	IECP	ANG	VEC	EC	
43312	43112	ae	IECP	ANG	VEC	EC	
43313	43113	ae	IECP	ANG	VEC	EC	
43314	43114	ae	IECP	ANG	VEC	EC	
43315	43115	ae	IECP	ANG	VEC	EC	
43316	43116	ae	IECP	ANG	VEC	EC	
43317	43117	ae	IECP	ANG	VEC	EC	
43318	43118	ae	IECP	ANG	VEC	EC	
43319	43119	ae	IECP	ANG	VEC	EC	
43320	43120	ae	IECP	ANG	VEC	EC	
43321	43121	ae	EHPC	POR	XCT	EC	
43357	43157	ae	EHPC	POR	XCT	EC	
43366	43166	ae	EHPC	ANG	XCT	EC	
43367	43167	ae	IECP	ANG	VEC	EC	*DELTIC 50 1955-2005*
43378	43178	ae	EHPC	ANG	XCT	EC	
43384	43184	ae	EHPC	ANG	XCT	EC	
43423	43123	aej	EMPC	ANG	EMU	NL	*VALENTA 1972-2010*

ScotRail has introduced short-form four-coach HST sets on many of its inter-city routes. Ex-GWR 43146 and 43169 pass Pettycur Bay, near Kinghorn with an Edinburgh-Aberdeen train on 10 May 2019. *Anthony Hicks*

On 6 April 2019, Arriva CrossCountry's 43378 brings up the rear of a Plymouth-Edinburgh train at Leeds.
Pip Dunn

43465	43065	aej	EMPC	ANG	EMU	NL	
43467	43068	aej	EMPC	ANG	EMR	NL	*British Transport Police Nottingham/ Nottinghamshire Fire and Rescue Service*
43468	43068	aej	EMPC	ANG	EMR	NL	
43480	43080	aej	EMPC	ANG	EMU	NL	*West Hampstead PB*
43484	43084	aej	EMPC	ANG	EMR	NL	

43274 has 'Spirit of Sunderland' branding

43295 has 'Perth is the Place' branding

43300 has 'Craigentinny 100 1914-2014' branding

Class 45

The development of the pilot scheme Class 44s, the last Class 45 was withdrawn in 1989. Since then, 45112 had a spell on the main line but is now stored. However, Locomotive Services has acquired 45118 and it is expected to return to the main line in the fullness of time.

Built by:	BR Crewe
Years introduced:	62
Wheel arrangement:	1Co-Co1
Weight:	135 tons
Length:	67ft 11in (20.7m)
Engine Type:	Sulzer 12LDA28B
Engine output:	2,500hp (1,865kW)
Power at rail:	2,000hp (1,592kW)
Tractive effort:	55,000lb (245kN)
Continuous tractive effort	30,000lbf (133kN)
Maximum design speed:	90mph (144km/h)
Brake Force:	63 tons
Route Availability:	7
Main generator type:	Crompton CG426A1
Auxiliary generator type:	Crompton CAG252A1
Traction Motor type:	Crompton C172A1
Fuel tank capacity:	840gal (3,780lit)
Multiple Working type	not fitted

| 45118 | D67 | xe | LSLS | LSL | BRB | BH (U) | *ROYAL ARTILLERYMAN* |

Class 47

BR's standard Type 4 diesel electric, 512 were built between 1962-68. Mass withdrawals started in 1986, but a few have found use with some private operators. Thirty-three were rebuilt as Class 57s. They remain the core loco for WCR and LSL while new TOC Vintage Trains has one loco and GBRf has three. LSL's 47853 carries the number 47614.

Built by:	Brush, Loughborough and BR Crewe
Years introduced:	1962-68
Wheel arrangement:	Co-Co
Weight:	111-121 tons
Length:	63ft 6in (19.38m)
Engine Type:	Sulzer 12LDA28C
Engine output:	2,580hp (1,922kW)
Power at rail:	2,080hp (1,550kW)
Tractive effort:	60,000lbf (267kN)
Continuous tractive effort	30,000lbf (133kN)
Maximum design speed:	95mph (152km/h)
Brake Force:	60 tons
Route Availability:	6
Main generator type:	Brush TG160-60 Mk 2, TG160-60 Mk 4 or TM172-50 Mk 1
Auxiliary generator type:	Brush TG69-20 or TG69-28 Mk 2
Traction Motor type:	Brush TM64-68 or TM64-68 Mk 1
Fuel tank capacity:	727 (3,273lit), t – 1,308gal (5,887lit)
Multiple Working type: (where fitted)	Green Circle

Class 47/0s – standard locos

47194	D1844	aotm	AWCX	WCR	RFD	CS (U)	
47237	D1914	xotm	AWCA	WCR	WCR	CS	
47245	D1922	xotmp*	AWCA	WCR	WCR	CS	
47270	D1971	ao	AWCA	WCR	BRB	CS (S)	*SWIFT*

Class 47/3 – originally built with no train heating

Details as per Class 47/0 except:
  Multiple Working type (where fitted): Green Circle

47355	D1836	aotm	AWCX	WCR	FRG	CS (U)
47368	D1887	xo		WCR	TTG	CS (U)

Class 47/4 – originally ETH fitted

Details as per Class 47/0 except:

ETH alternator type:	Brush BL100-30
ETH index:	66
Fuel tank capacity:	727 (3,273lit), t – 1,230gal (5,537lit)
Multiple Working type: (where fitted)	DRS system

47492	D1760	xe	AWCX	WCR	RES	CS (U)	
47501	D1944	aetm	LSLO	LSL	GYP	CD	*CRAFTSMAN*
47526	D1109	xe		WCR	LLB	CS (U)	
47580	D1762, 47167, 47732	xet	MBDL	SFG	BRF	CS (U)	*County of Essex*
47593	D1973, 47272, 47673, 47790	aetmp*	LSLO	LSL	BLL	CD	*Galloway Princess*

Note: 47580 is RA7

Class 47/7 – original ScR push-pull

Details as per Class 47/4

47712	D1948, 47505	xet	MBDL	D05	SCR	CD (S)	Lady Diana Spencer

Class 47/7 – Converted locos for Rail Express Systems

Details as per Class 47/4

Multiple Working type: Green Circle or DRS system (47790)
(where fitted)

47727	D1629, 47047, 47569	aetmd	GBDF	GBR	CAL	RR	Edinburgh Castle/Caisteal Dhùn Èideann
47739	D1615, 47035, 47594	aetmd	GBDF	GBU	GBB	RR	
47746	D1754, 47160, 47605	xet	AWCA	WCR	WCR	CS	Chris Fudge 29.7.70-22.6.10
47749	D1660, 47076, 47625	aetmd	GBDF	GBR	BRB	RR	CITY OF TRURO
47760	D1617, 47036, 47562, 47672	xetp*	AWCA	WCR	WCR	BU (U)	
47768	D1725, 47490	aet	AWCX	WCR	UND	CS (U)	
47772	D1657, 47537	xet	AWCA	WCR	WCR	CS (U)	Carnforth TMD
47773	D1755, 47541	xetp	MBDL	VIN	GYP	TM	
47776	D1776, 47181, 47578	xet	AWCX	WCR	RES	CS (U)	
47786	D1730, 47138, 47607, 47821	aet	AWCA	WCR	WCR	CS (U)	Roy Castle OBE
47787	D1757, 47163, 47610, 47823	aet	AWCX	WCR	WCR	CS (U)	
47798	D1656, 47072, 47609, 47834	xet	MBDL	NRM	RTP	YK (S)	Prince William

Note: 47727/739/749 have an extra jumper receptacle on their cab fronts to allow them to haul new Bombardier EMUs

Class 47/4 continued

Multiple Working type: Green Circle (47812/815/843/847/848) or DRS system
(where fitted)   (47802/805/813/832/841)

47802	D1950, 47552	xetm	AWCA	WCR	WCR	CS	
47804	D1965, 47265, 47591, 47792	xet	AWCA	WCR	WCR	CS	
47805	D1935, 47257, 47650	aetm	LSLO	LSL	GYP	CD	Roger Hosking MA 1925-2013
47810	D1924, 47247, 47655	aetm	LSLO	LSL	GYP	CD	Crewe Diesel Depot
47811	D1719, 47128, 47656	aet	DHLT	LSL	FPG	CD (U)	
47812	D1916, 47239, 47657	aetm	GROG	ROG	OXB	ZG (U)	
47813	D1720, 47129, 47658	aetmp*	GROG	ROG	ROG	LR	Jack Frost
47815	D1748, 47155, 47660	aetm	GROG	ROG	ROG	LR	Lost Boys 68-88
47816	D1650, 47066, 47661	aet	DHLT	LSL	FPG	CD (U)	
47818	D1917, 47240, 47663	aetm	MBDL	AFS	DRU	ZG (U)	
47826	D1976, 47274, 47637	aet	AWCA	WCR	WCR	CS	

Rail Operations Group has two active main line Class 47s plus several in strategic reserve. On 7 April, 47813 *Jack Frost* and 47815 *Lost Boys 68-88* pass Ashwell moving a rake of redundant ex-GWR HST trailers from Plymouth for store at Ely. *Bill Atkinson*

Locomotive Services Limited's 47593 *Galloway Princess* waits to depart with 1Z63, the 1130 Mallaig-Fort William 'Statesman' charter on 24 March 2019. On the rear is 47501 *Craftsman*. *Mark Hare*

47828	D1966, 47266, 47629	aet	AWCA	DO5	ICS	CS	
47830	D1645, 47061, 47649	aet	DFLH	FLI	GYP	CB	*BEECHING'S LEGACY*
47832	D1610, 47031, 47560	aetm	AWCA	WCR	WCR	CS	
47841	D1726, 47134, 47622	aetm	LSLS	LSL	ICS	MR (U)	
47843	D1676, 47090, 47623	aetm	SROG	ROG	OXB	LR (U)	
47847	D1774, 47179, 47577	aetm	SROG	ROG	LLB	LR (U)	
47848	D1652, 47068, 47632	aetm	SROG	ROG	OXB	IL (U)	
47851	D1648, 47064, 47639	aet	AWCA	WCR	WCR	CS	
47853	D1733, 47141, 47614	aetm	LSLO	LSL	BRB	CD	
47854	D1972, 47271, 47604, 47674	aetp*	AWCA	WCR	WCR	CS	*Diamond Jubilee*

Note: 47853 carries the number 47614

Class 50

A fleet of 50 Type 4 diesel electrics built in 1967/68 and withdrawn by 1994. The main line survivors are essentially preserved but do find spot hire use. Two have recently been repainted into GBRf livery while 50008 is a regular sport hire loco working for various FOCs. No. 50007 carries the number and name 50014 Warspite on one side but this may change to another loco's identity.

Built by:	English Electric Vulcan Foundry
Years introduced:	1967-68
Wheel arrangement:	Co-Co
Weight:	117 tons
Length:	68ft 6in (20.87m)
Engine Type:	English Electric 16CSVT

No. 50008 *Thunderer* is owned by Hanson Traction and hired to main line operators as required. On 2 April 2019 it made a very rare appearance for a Class 50 at Spalding as it passes with a rake of redundant hopper wagons. *Pip Dunn*

Engine output:	2,700hp (2,014kW)
Power at rail:	2,070hp (1,540kW)
Tractive effort:	48,500lbf (216kN)
Continuous tractive effort	33,000lbf (147kN)
ETH generator type:	EE915-1B
ETH index:	61
Maximum design speed:	100mph (160km/h)
Brake Force:	59 tons
Route Availability:	6
Main generator type:	EE840-4B
Auxiliary generator type:	EE911-5C
Traction Motor type:	EE538-5A
Fuel tank capacity:	1,055gal (4,797lit)
Multiple Working type:	Orange Square

50007	D407	xep	CFOL	CFA	GBR	KR	*Hercules*
50008	D408	xep	HTLX	GAR	LAB	LR	*Thunderer*
50044	D444	xep	CFOL	CFA	BRB	KR	*Exeter*
50049	D449, 50149	xep*	CFOL	CFA	GBR	KR	*Defiance*
50050	D400	xep	BREL	BOD	BRB	NE	*Fearless*

Class 52

Type 4 diesel hydraulic design, with 74 locos built but all withdrawn by 1977. The sole main line survivor, one of seven which are preserved, is used mostly on occasional charter trains and is not in day-to-day use. It has been under repairs for the last two years but is expected to return to traffic in 2020.

Built by:	BR Swindon or Crewe
Years introduced:	1961-64
Wheel arrangement:	C-C
Weight:	108 tons
Length:	68ft (20.73m)
Engine Type:	two Maybach MD655
Total Engine output:	2,700hp (2,014kW)
Power at rail:	2,350hp (1,753kW)
Tractive effort:	66,700lbf (297kN)
Continuous tractive effort	45,200lbf (201kN)
Maximum design speed:	90mph (144km/h)
Brake Force:	82 tons
Route Availability:	6
Transmission type:	Voith L630rU
Fuel tank capacity:	850gal (3,825lit)
Multiple Working type:	None

D1015	xo	MBDL	DTG	BYP	KR	*WESTERN CHAMPION*

Class 55

An English Electric twin-engine Type 5 passenger design, just 22 were built for ECML work. All were withdrawn by 1982. Six survivors are preserved but see occasional spot hire use. No. 55009 is currently main line registered but has been stopped for major repairs.

Built by:	English Electric, Vulcan Foundry
Years introduced:	1961-62

Class 55 Deltic D9009 *Alycidon* leads 68004 Rapid past Billingham, near Stockton-on-Tees, with the 0608 Willington-Carlisle charter on 29 September 2018. *Anthony Hicks*

Wheel arrangement:	Co-Co
Weight:	100 tons
Length:	69ft 6in (21.18m)
Engine Type:	two Napier D18-25 'Deltic'
Engine output:	3,300hp (2,460kW)
Power at rail:	2,460hp (1,969kW)
Tractive effort:	50,000lbf (222kN)
Continuous tractive effort	30,500lbf (136kN)
ETH index:	66
Maximum design speed:	100mph (160km/h)
Brake Force:	51 tons
Route Availability:	5
Main generator type:	two English Electric EE829-1A
Auxiliary generator type:	two English Electric EE913-1A
Traction Motor type:	English Electric EE538A
Fuel tank capacity:	826gal (3,717lit), 1,626gal (7,317lit) – 55022
Multiple Working type:	None

55002	D9002	xe	DBLX	NRM	GYP	YK (S)	THE KING'S OWN YORKSHIRE LIGHT INFANTRY
55009	D9009	xe	DBLX	DPS	BRB	BU (U)	ALYCIDON
55016	D9016	xei	LSLS	LSL	GYE	CD (U)	GORDON HIGHLANDER
55022	D9000	xet	LSLS	LSL	BRB	CD (U)	ROYAL SCOTS GREY

Colas Rail Freight's 56087/105 work 6E32, the 1002 Preston Docks-Lindsey, past Godnow Bridge, between Thorne and Scunthorpe, on 17 May 2019. *Anthony Hicks*

Class 56

Type 5 freight loco built from 1976 to 1984. The first 30 locos were built in Romania, with the remainder built at Doncaster and Crewe. Withdrawn by EWS in March 2004, a few have found use with spot hire companies, DC Rail and Colas Rail Freight. GB Railfreight has recently bought 18 locos, of which most will be rebuilt as Class 69s with GM engines.

Built by:	Electroputere in Craiovia Romania, BREL Doncaster and Crewe
Years introduced:	1976-84
Wheel arrangement:	Co-Co
Weight:	126 tons
Length:	63ft 6in (19.39m)
Engine Type:	Ruston Paxman 16RK3CT
Engine output:	3,250hp (2,420kW)
Power at rail:	2,400hp (1,790kW)
Tractive effort:	61,800lbf (275kN)
Continuous tractive effort	53,950lbf (240kN)
Maximum design speed:	80mph (128km/h)
Brake Force:	60 tons
Route Availability:	7
Main alternator type:	Brush BA1101A
Auxiliary alternator type:	Brush BAA602A
Traction Motor type:	Brush TMH73-62
Fuel tank capacity:	1,150gal (5,228lit)
Multiple Working type:	Red Diamond

DC Rail's two operational Class 56s are both now in the company's grey livery. On 15 May 2019, 56103 leads 56091 past Great Hale Drove with 6Z57, the 1351 Boston Sleaford Sidings-Carlisle Kingmoor VQ ballast empties. *Bill Atkinson*

56007	aos	UKRS	GBR	DCR	ZW (U)	
56009	aos		GBR	BLE	ZW (U)	
56018	aos	UKRS	GBR	FER	ZW (U)	
56031	aos	GBGS	GBR	FER	ZW (U)	
56032	aos	GBGS	GBR	FER	ZW (U)	
56037	aos	GBGS	GBR	EWS	ZW (U)	
56038	aos	UKRS	GBR	FER	ZW (U)	
56049	aos	COFS	BEA	COL	RU	*Robin of Templecombe 1938-2013*
56051	aos	COLS	BEA	COL	NE (U)	
56060	aos	UKRS	GBR	FER	ZW (U)	
56065	aos	UKRS	GBR	FER	ZW (U)	
56069	aos	GBGS	GBR	FER	ZW (U)	
56077	aos	UKRS	GBR	LHO	ZW (U)	
56078	aos	COFS	BEA	COL	RU	
56081	aos	GBGD	GBR	UKG	HQ	
56087	aos	COFS	BEA	COL	RU	
56090	aos	COFS	BEA	COL	RU	
56091	aos	HTLX	UKR	DCN	LR	*Driver Wayne Gaskell The Godfather*
56094	aos	COFS	BEA	COL	RU	
56096	aos	COFS	BEA	COL	RU	
56098	aos	GBGD	GBR	RFO	HQ	
56103	aos	HTLX	UKR	DCN	LR	
56104	aos	UKRL	GBR	UKG	LR (S)	
56105	aos	COFS	BEA	COL	RU	
56106	aos	UKRS	GBR	UKG	LR (U)	
56113	aos	COFS	BEA	COL	NE	

56128		aos		GBR	TRN	ZW (U)	
56301	56045	aos	UKRL	CFS	JFU	HQ	
56302	56124	aosr	COFS	BEA	COL	RU	*PECO The Railway Modeller 2016 70 years*
56303	56125	aos	HTLX	UKR	DCG	WN (U)	
56311	56057	aos	GBGS	GBR	FER	ZW (U)	
56312	56003	aos	GBGD	GBR	DCR	ZW (U)	

Class 57

Brush-built locos using the bodies and bogies from redundant Class 47s and re-engineered with second-hand GM engines. Initial order was with Freightliner, for up to 30 locos, but cut back to 12. No. 57601 was a demonstrator ETH version, later sold to WCR while Virgin Trains ordered 16 and First Great Western four. The fleet is now split between DRS, GWR and WCR with two DRS locos on long-term hire to the Rail Operations Group.

Rebuilt by:	Brush Traction
Years introduced:	1998-99
Wheel arrangement:	Co-Co
Weight:	121 tons
Length:	63ft 6in (19.38m)
Engine Type:	General Motors 645-12E3
Engine output:	2,500hp (1,860kW)
Power at rail:	2,025hp (1,507kW)
Tractive effort:	55,000lbf (245kN)
Continuous tractive effort	31,500lbf (140kN)
Maximum design speed:	75mph (121km/h)
Brake Force:	80 tons
Route Availability:	6
Main alternator type:	Brush BA1101A
Auxiliary alternator type:	Brush BAA602A
Traction Motor type:	Brush TM68-46
Fuel tank capacity:	1,221gal (5,550lit)
Multiple Working type:	Green Circle (where fitted)

Class 57/0 – original locos built for Freightliner without train heating

57001	D1875, 47356	ao	AWCA	WCR	WCR	CS	
57002	D1803, 47322	aom	XHCK	DRS	DRN	KM	*RAIL Express*
57003	D1798, 47317	aom	XHCK	DRS	DRN	KM	
57004	D1828, 47347	aom	XHSS	DRS	DRC	LT (S)	
57005	D1831, 47350	ao	AWCX	WCR	ADZ	CS (U)	
57006	D1837, 47187	ao	AWCX	WCR	WCR	CS	
57007	D1813, 47332	aom	XHCK	DRS	DRN	KM	*John Scott 12.5.45-22.5.12*
57008	D1644, 47060	aom	XHSS	DRS	DRC	LT (S)	
57009	D1664, 47079	aom	XHSS	DRS	DRC	LT (S)	
57010	D1907, 47231	aom	XHSS	DRS	DRN	LT (S)	
57011	D1810, 47329	aom	XHSS	DRS	DRC	LT (U)	
57012	D1854, 47204	aom	XHSS	DRS	DRC	LT (S)	

Class 57/3 – ETH locos originally ordered by Virgin trains

Years introduced	2002-04
Engine Type:	General Motors 645-12F3B
Engine output:	2,750hp (2,051kW)
Power at rail:	2,200hp (1,640kW)

Weight:	117 tons
Main alternator type:	Brush BA1101F or BA1101G
ETH alternator type:	Brush BAA
ETH index:	100
Maximum design speed:	95mph (153km/h)
Brake Force:	60 tons
Fuel tank capacity:	1,308gal (5,887lit)
Multiple Working type:	None

57301	D1653, 47069, 47638, 47845	aedr	XHAC	POR	DRN	KM	*Goliath*
57302	D1928, 47251, 47589, 47827	aed	XHSS	DRS	DRC	ZG (S)	*Chad Varah*
57303	D1957, 47554, 47705	aed	XHAC	POR	DRN	KM	*Pride of Carlisle*
57304	D1639, 47055, 47652, 47807	aed	XHVT	DRS	DRN	KM	*Pride of Cheshire*
57305	D1758, 47164, 47571, 47822	aed	GROG	POR	NOB	LR	*Northern Princess*
57306	D1919, 47242, 47659, 47814	aed	XHAC	POR	DRN	KM	*Her Majesty's Railway Inspectorate 175*
57307	D1901, 47225	aed	XHVT	DRS	DRN	KM	*LADY PENELOPE*
57308	D1677, 47091, 47647, 47846	aed	XHVT	DRS	DRN	KM	*James Ferguson*
57309	D1931, 47254, 47651, 47806	aed	XHVT	DRS	DRN	KM	*Pride of Crewe*
57310	D1618, 47037, 47563, 47831	aedr	XHAC	POR	DRN	KM	*Pride of Cumbria*
57311	D1611, 47032, 47662, 47817	aed	XHSS	DRS	DRC	LT (S)	*Thunderbird*
57312	D1811, 47330	aedr	GROG	POR	NOB	LR	*Solway Princess*
57313	D1890, 47371	ae	AWCA	WCR	NOB	CS	
57314	D1891, 47372	ae	AWCA	WCR	WCR	CS	
57315	D1911, 47234	ae	AWCA	WCR	WCR	CS	
57316	D1992, 47290	ae	AWCA	WCR	WCR	CS	

57307 has '20 years of Direct Rail Services' branding
57305/312 are on sub lease to ROG

Class 57/6 – Locos fitted with ETH

Details as per Class 57/3 except:

Years introduced	2001
Weight:	113 tons
Main alternator type:	Brush BA1101E
ETH index:	95
Fuel tank capacity:	727gal (3,273lit)

57601	D1759, 47165, 47590, 47825	ae	AWCA	WCR	NOB	CS	*Windsor Castle*
57602	D1818, 47337	aep*	EFOO	POR	GWT	OO	*Restormel Castle*
57603	D1830, 47349	aep*	EFOO	POR	GWT	OO	*Tintagel Castle*
57604	D1859, 47209	aep*	EFOO	POR	GWR	OO	*PENDENNIS CASTLE*
57605	D1856, 47206	aep*	EFOO	POR	GWT	OO	*Totnes Castle*

Skirting the west side of Rutland Water, 57305 *Northern Princess* and 37611 *Pegasus* top-and-tail 5Q72, the 1341 Old Dalby-Willesden delivery run with a Class 345 unit, passing Ashwell. *Bill Atkinson*

Class 59

The first four Class 59/0s, owned by Foster Yeoman, were the first privately owned main line diesels to run on BR, in 1986. FY later ordered a fifth loco while ARC ordered four 59/1s, which were delivered in 1990, and National Power ordered six Class 59/2s. The latter are now owned by DB Cargo. No. 59003 spent 1997-2014 in Germany until bought by GB Railfreight. Following a change to traction provider for Mendip stine trains, 59001/002/004/005/101-104 have recently passed to Freightliner ownership. Nos 59201-206 were all offered for sale by tender in June 2019 by DB Cargo and acquired by Freigthliner.

Built by:	GM-EMD, La Grange, Illinois, USA
Years introduced:	1985-95
Wheel arrangement:	Co-Co
Weight:	121 tons
Length:	70ft (21.40m)
Engine Type:	EMD 16-645E3C
Engine output:	3,000hp (2,238kW)
Power at rail:	2,533hp (1,889kW)
Tractive effort:	113,550lbf (506kN)
Continuous tractive effort	65,300lbf (291kN)
Maximum design speed:	60mph (96km/h)
Brake Force:	69 tons
Route Availability:	7
Traction alternator:	EMD AR11
Companion alternator:	EMD D14A

Auxiliary alternator:	EMD 3A8147
Traction Motor type:	EMD D77B
Fuel tank capacity:	1,000gal (4,546lit)
Multiple Working type:	AAR

Class 59/0 – original Foster Yeoman locos

59001	aos	XYPO	FHH	AGI	MD	YEOMAN ENDEAVOUR
59002	aos	XYPO	FHH	AGI	MD	ALAN J DAY
59003	aos	GBYH	GBR	GBR	RR	YEOMAN HIGHLANDER
59004	aos	XYPO	FHH	AGI	MD	PAUL A HAMMOND
59005	aos	XYPO	FHH	AGI	MD	KENNETH J PAINTER

Class 59/1 – original ARC locos

59101	aos	XYPA	FHH	HAN	MD	Village of Whatley
59102	aos	XYPA	FHH	HAN	MD	Village of Chantry
59103	aos	XYPA	FHH	HAN	MD	Village of Mells
59104	aos	XYPA	FHH	HAN	MD	Village of Great Elm

Class 59/2 – original National Power locos

59201	aos	WDAM	FHH	DBC	MD	
59202	aos	WDAM	FHH	DBC	MD	Alan Meddows Taylor MD Mendip Rail Limited
59203	aos	WDAM	FHH	DBC	MD	
59204	aos	WDAM	FHH	DBC	MD	
59205	aos	WDAM	FHH	DBC	MD	
59206	aos	WDAM	FHH	DBC	MD	John F Yeoman Rail Pioneer

GB Railfreight acquired 59003 *Yeoman Highlander* in 2014 from a German operator and returned it to the UK. On 26 February 2019, the loco was at Westbury. *Mark Pike*

The first four Class 59s delivered to Foster Yeoman in UK are now nearly 34 years old but are still working. Now in Aggregates Industries livery, 59004 *Paul A Hammond* passes West Ealing on 1 April 2019. *Paul Shannon*

Class 60

Heavy freight Type 5 built by Brush, the last diesel locos delivered to BR. All were inherited by EWS (Now DB Cargo). The fleet has been steadily run down since 2004 with ten locos sold to Colas Rail Freight and since resold to GBRf, which has also acquired locos for spares. DC Rail's parent company has recently bought four locos, which are being overhauled by DB Cargo at Toton, and more could follow. DBC retains a fluctuating fleet of about 20 overhauled locos.

Nos 60006/050/060/081/086 were offered for sale by tender by DB Cargo as this book closed for press, but are expected to go for scrap.

Built by:	Brush Traction, Loughborough
Years introduced:	1989-93
Wheel arrangement:	Co-Co
Weight:	129-130 tons
Length:	70ft (21.34m)
Engine Type:	Mirrlees MB275T
Engine output:	3,100hp (2,240kW)
Power at rail:	2,415hp (1,800kW)
Tractive effort:	106,500lbf (500kN)
Continuous tractive effort	71,570lbf (336kN)
Maximum design speed:	62mph (99km/h)
Brake Force:	74 tons
Route Availability:	7
Main alternator type:	Brush BA1000

Auxiliary alternator type:		Brush BAA700			
Traction Motor type:		Brush TM216			
Fuel tank capacity:		990gal (4,500lit)			
Multiple Working type:		Within Class only			

Number	Code	A	B	C	D	Name
60001	aos	WCAT	DBC	DBC	TO	
60002	aost	GBTG	BEA	COL	RS	
60003	aost	WQDA	DBC	EWS	TY (U)	FREIGHT TRANSPORT ASSOCIATION
60004	aost	WQDA	GBR	EWS	TO (U)	
60005	aost	WQDA	DBC	EWS	TY (U)	
60006	aos	WQDA	DBC	COR	TO (U)	
60007	aost	WCBT	DBC	DBC	TO	The Spirit of Tom Kendall
60008	aos	WQDA	DBC	EWS	TC (U)	Sir William McAlpine
60009	aost	WQBA	DBC	EWS	TC (U)	
60010	aost	WQAA	DBC	DBC	TO (S)	
60011	aos	WCAT	DBC	DBC	TO	
60012	aost	WQBA	DBC	EWS	TC (U)	
60013	aos	WQDA	DBC	TEW	TC (U)	Robert Boyle
60014	aos	WQDA	GBR	TEW	TO (U)	
60015	aost	WCBT	DBC	DBU	TO	
60017	aost	WCBT	DBC	DBC	TO	
60018	aos	WQDA	GBR	EWS	TY (U)	
60019	aos	WCAT	DBC	DBC	TO	Port of Grimsby & Immingham
60020	aost	WCBT	DBC	DBC	TO	The Willows
60021	aost	GBTG	BEA	GBR	RS	PENYGHENT
60022	aost	WQDA	DBC	EWS	TO (U)	
60023	aost	WQDA	DBC	EWS	TY (U)	
60024	aos	WCAT	DBC	DBC	TO	Clitheroe Castle
60025	aost	WQDA	DBC	EWS	TY (U)	
60026	aost	GBTG	BEA	BEA	RS	HELVELLYN
60027	aost	WQDA	DBC	EWS	TY (U)	
60028	aost	WQAA	CAP	TEW	TO (U)	
60029	aos	WQAA	CAP	EWS	TO (U)	
60030	aost	WQDA	DBC	EWS	TO (U)	
60031	aos	WQDA	DBC	EWS	TY (U)	
60032	aos	WQDA	DBC	TRN	TY (U)	
60033	aost	WQCA	DBC	COR	TC (U)	Tees Steel Express
60034	aos	WQBA	DBC	TEW	TO (U)	Carnedd Llewelyn
60035	aos	WQBA	DBC	EWS	TO (U)	
60036	aos	WQBA	DBC	EWS	TO (U)	GEFCO
60037	aost	WQDA	DBC	EWS	TY (U)	
60038	aost	WQCA	DBC	EWS	TO (U)	
60039	aos	WCAT	DBC	DBC	TO	Dove Holes
60040	aos	WCAT	DBC	DBC	TO	The Territorial Army Centenary
60041	aost	WQCA	DBC	EWS	TC (U)	
60042	aos	WQDA	DBC	EWS	TY (U)	
60043	aos	WQBA	DBC	EWS	TO (U)	
60044	aos	WCAT	DBC	DBC	TO	Dowlow
60045	aos	WQBA	DBC	EWS	TC (U)	The Permanent Way Institution
60046	aost	WQAA	CAP	TEW	TO (U)	
60047	aos	GBTG	BEA	COL	PG	
60048	aos	WQCA	DBC	EWS	TO (U)	
60049	aos	WQBA	DBC	EWS	TO (U)	
60050	aos	WQDA	DBC	EWS	TO (U)	

GB Railfreight 60095 works 6N20, the 1754 Drax-Tyne, past Sherburn-in-Elmet on 24 May 2019. The 10 GBRf Class 60s are in the process of being named after the original 10 Class 44 Peaks. *Anthony Hicks*

60051	aost	WQDA	DBC	EWS	TO (U)	
60052	aost	WQDA	DBC	EWS	TO (U)	*Glofa Tŵr The last deep mine in Wales Tower Colliery*
60053	aos	WQBA	DBC	EWS	TY (U)	
60054	aost	WCBT	DBC	DBC	TO	
60055	aost	WQAA	CAP	TEW	TO (U)	
60056	aost	GBTG	BEA	COL	PG	
60057	aos	WQBA	DBC	TEW	TO (U)	*Adam Smith*
60058	aost	WQBA	DBC	EWS	TO (U)	
60059	aost	WCBT	DBC	DBC	TO	*Swinden Dalesman*
60060	aos	WQBA	DBC	TEW	TY (U)	
60061	aos	WQCA	DBC	TRN	TC (U)	
60062	aos	WCAT	DBC	DBC	TO	*Stainless Pioneer*
60063	aos	WCAT	DBC	DBC	TO	
60064	aost	WQBA	DBC	TEW	TO (U)	*Back Tor*
60065	aos	WCAT	DBC	EWS	TO	*SPIRIT OF JAGUAR*
60066	aos	WCAT	DBC	DRA	TO	
60067	aos	WQBA	DBC	TEW	TY (U)	
60068	aos	WQBA	DBC	TEW	TO (U)	
60069	aos	WQBA	DBC	EWS	TC (U)	*Slioch*
60070	aost	WQBA	DBC	TLH	TO (U)	
60071	aost	WQBA	DBC	EWS	TO (U)	*Ribblehead Viaduct*
60072	aos	WQBA	DBC	TEW	TC (U)	
60073	aos	WQBA	DBC	TEW	TO (U)	*Cairn Gorm*
60074	aos	WCAT	DBC	DBC	TO	
60075	aos	WQBA	DBC	EWS	TC (U)	
60076	aos	GBTG	BEA	COL	PG	

DB Cargo has a fleet of about 20 active Class 60s, although not all are in traffic at any one time. No. 60039 *Doves Holes* passes Acton Bridge on 5 May 2017. *Paul Shannon*

60077		aost	WQBA	DBC	TEW	TC (U)	
60078		aos	WQBA	DBC	MEW	TY (U)	
60079		aos	WQAB	DBC	DBC	TO (U)	
60080		aost	WQBA	DBC	EWS	TO (U)	
60081		aost	WQBA	DBC	GWR	TY (U)	
60082		aos	WQBA	DBC	TEW	CE (U)	
60083		aos	WQBA	DBC	EWS	TY (U)	
60084		aos	WQBA	DBC	TEW	TC (U)	
60085		aos	GBTG	BEA	COL	PG	
60086		aos	WQBA	DBC	TEW	TY (U)	
60087		aos	GBTG	BEA	COL	PG	
60088		aos	WQBA	DBC	TEW	TY (U)	
60089		aost	WQBA	DBC	EWS	TY (U)	
60090		aost	WQBA	DBC	TEW	TC (U)	
60091		aost	WCBT	DBC	DBC	TO	*Barry Needham*
60092		aost	WCBT	DBC	DBC	TO	
60093		aos	WQBA	DBC	EWS	TY (U)	
60094		aos	WQBA	DBC	EWS	TC (U)	*Rugby Flyer*
60095		aos	GBTG	BEA	GBR	PG	
60096		aost	GBTG	BEA	COL	PG	
60097		aost	WQBA	DBC	EWS	TY (U)	
60098		aost	WQBA	DBC	EWS	TO (U)	
60099		aos	WQBA	DBC	TAS	TO (U)	
60100		aos	WCAT	DBC	DBC	TO	*Midland Railway – Butterley*
60500	60016	aos	WQBA	DBC	EWS	TO (U)	

60007 has 'SWITCH ON TO SAFETY' branding

Class 66

EWS ordered 250 locos in 1996, which were delivered in 1998-2000, and since then Freightliner, GBRf, DRS and Fastline Freight (now defunct) placed orders. DBC has moved many locos to France and Poland, while Freightliner has also redeployed some locos to Poland. Some have been renumbered and three written off. GBRf has recently bought three more locos from Europe, and others could follow if they become available. Five DB Cargo locos are on long term hire to DRS, and five more locos may be added to this deal.

Built by:	General Motors, London, Canada or EMD Muncie, Indiana, USA
Years introduced:	1998-2000
Wheel arrangement:	Co-Co
Weight:	126 tons
Length:	70ft 1in (21.40m)
Engine Type:	GM 12N-710G3B-EC
Engine output:	3,300hp (2,462kW)
Power at rail:	3,000hp (2,238kW)
Maximum tractive effort:	92,000lbf (409kN)
Continuous tractive effort:	58,390lbf (260kN)
Maximum design speed:	75mph (120km/h)
Brake Force:	68 tons
Route Availability:	7
Traction alternator:	GM-EMD AR8
Companion alternator:	GM-EMD CA6
Traction Motor type:	GM-EMD D43TR
Fuel tank capacity:	1,440gal (6,550lit)
Multiple Working type:	AAR

Class 66/0 – locos ordered by EWS (Now DB Cargo)

66001	aosck	WBAE	DBC	DBS	TO	
66002	aos	WBAE	DBC	EWS	TO	
66003	aos	WBAE	DBC	EWS	TO	
66004	aosk	WBAR	DBC	EWS	TO	
66005	aos	WBAE	DBC	MRD	TO	*Maritime Intermodal One*
66006	aos	WBAR	DBC	EWS	TO	
66007	aoskq	WBAR	DBC	EWS	TO	
66009	aosk	WBAE	DBC	DBC	TO	
66011	aosk	WBAE	DBC	EWS	TO	
66012	aosk	WBAE	DBC	EWS	TO	
66013	aosk	WBAE	DBC	EWS	TO	
66014	aosk	WBAR	DBC	EWS	TO	
66015	aosk	WBAR	DBC	EWS	TO	
66017	aosckq	WBAR	DBC	DBS	TO	
66018	aosk	WBAE	DBC	DBC	TO	
66019	aosckq	WBAR	DBC	EWS	TO	
66020	aosk	WBAE	DBC	DBC	TO	
66021	aoskq	WBAR	DBC	DBC	TO	
66023	aos	WBAT	DBC	EWS	TO	
66024	aosk	WBAE	DBC	EWS	TO	
66025	aoskq	WBAR	DBC	EWS	TO	
66027	aos	WBAE	DBC	DBC	TO	
66030	aosq	WBAR	DBC	EWS	TO	
66031	aos	XHIM	DBC	EWS	KM	
66034	aosk	WBAE	DBC	DBC	TO	

66035	aosk	WBAE	DBC	DBC	TO	Resourceful
66037	aoskq	WBAR	DBC	EWS	TO	
66039	aosk	WBAE	DBC	EWS	TO	
66040	aoskq	WBRT	DBC	EWS	TO	
66041	aosk	WBAR	DBC	DBC	TO	
66043	aosk	WQBA	DBC	EWS	TO (U)	
66044	aosk	WBAE	DBC	DBC	TO	
66047	aos	WBAE	DBC	MRD	TO	Maritime Intermodal Two
66050	aosk	WBAE	DBC	EWS	TO	EWS Energy
66051	aoskq	WBAR	DBC	MRD	TO	Maritime Intermodal Four
66053	aosk	WBAE	DBC	EWS	TO	
66054	aoskq	WBAR	DBC	EWS	TO	
66055	aoshkq	WBAR	DBC	DBC	TO	Alain Thauvette
66056	aoshk	WBLE	DBC	EWS	TO	
66057	aoshk	WBLE	DBC	EWS	TO	
66059	aoshk	WBLE	DBC	EWS	TO	
66060	aos	WBAR	DBC	EWS	TO	
66061	aosk	WBRT	DBC	EWS	TO	
66063	aosk	WBAE	DBC	EWS	TO	
66065	aoskq	WBAR	DBC	DBC	TO	
66066	aoskq	WBAR	DBC	DBC	TO	Geoff Spencer
66067	aoskq	WBAR	DBC	EWS	TO	
66068	aosk	WBAR	DBC	EWS	TO	
66069	aosq	WBRT	DBC	EWS	TO	
66070	aos	WBAT	DBC	DBC	TO	
66074	aosk	WBAE	DBC	DBC	TO	
66075	aos	WBAE	DBC	EWS	TO	
66076	aosk	WBAE	DBC	EWS	TO	
66077	aoskq	WBAR	DBC	DBC	TO	Benjamin Gimbert G.C.
66078	aosk	WBAE	DBC	DBC	TO	
66079	aosq	WBRT	DBC	EWS	TO	James Nightall G.C.
66080	aosk	WBAE	DBC	EWS	TO	
66082	aosk	WBAE	DBC	DBC	TO	
66083	aoskq	WBAR	DBC	EWS	TO	
66084	aosk	WBAR	DBC	EWS	TO	
66085	aoskq	WBRT	DBC	DBC	TO	
66086	aos	WBRT	DBC	EWS	TO	
66087	aosk	WBAE	DBC	EWS	TO	
66088	aosk	WBAE	DBC	EWS	TO	
66089	aoskq	WBAR	DBC	EWS	TO	
66090	aosk	WBAE	DBC	EWS	TO	
66091	aosk	XHIM	DBC	EWS	KM	
66092	aosk	WBAE	DBC	EWS	TO	
66093	aosk	WBAE	DBC	EWS	TO	
66094	aosk	WBAE	DBC	EWS	TO	
66095	aosk	WBAE	DBC	EWS	TO	
66096	aosk	WBAR	DBC	EWS	TO	
66097	aosk	WBAE	DBC	DBS	TO	
66098	aosk	WBAE	DBC	EWS	TO	
66099	aosrk	WBBE	DBC	EWS	TO	
66100	aosrk	WBBE	DBC	DBC	TO	Armistice 100 1918-2018
66101	aosrk	WBBE	DBC	DBS	TO	
66102	aosrk	WBBE	DBC	EWS	TO	
66103	aosrk	WBBE	DBC	EWS	TO	
66104	aosrkq	WBBT	DBC	DBC	TO	
66105	aosrk	WBAR	DBC	DBC	TO	
66106	aosrk	WBBE	DBC	EWS	TO	
66107	aosrkq	WBBT	DBC	DBC	TO	

66108	aosrk	XHIM	DBC	EWS	KM	
66109	aosq	WBAR	DBC	PDP	TO	
66110	aosrk	WBBE	DBC	EWS	TO	
66111	aosr	WBBE	DBC	EWS	TO	
66112	aosrk	WBBE	DBC	EWS	TO	
66113	aosrk	WBBE	DBC	DBC	TO	
66114	aosrk	WBBT	DBC	DBS	TO	
66115	aos	WBAE	DBC	EWS	TO	
66116	aosk	WBAE	DBC	EWS	TO	
66117	aosk	WBAE	DBC	DBC	TO	
66118	aosk	WBAE	DBC	DBS	TO	
66119	aosk	WBAE	DBC	EWS	TO	
66120	aosk	WBAE	DBC	EWS	TO	
66121	aosk	WBAE	DBC	EWS	TO	
66122	aosk	XHIM	DBC	EWS	KM	
66124	aoskq	WBAR	DBC	DBC	TO	
66125	aosk	WBAE	DBC	EWS	TO	
66126	aosk	XHIM	DBC	EWS	KM	
66127	aos	WBAT	DBC	EWS	TO	
66128	aosk	WBAE	DBC	DBC	TO	
66129	aoskq	WBAR	DBC	EWS	TO	
66130	aoskq	WBAR	DBC	DBC	TO	
66131	aos	WBAE	DBC	DBC	TO	
66133	aosk	WBAE	DBC	EWS	TO	
66134	aosk	WBAE	DBC	DBC	TO	
66135	aosk	WBAE	DBC	DBC	TO	
66136	aoskq	WBAE	DBC	DBC	TO	
66137	aosk	WBRT	DBC	EWS	TO	
66138	aoskq	WQAB	DBC	EWS	TO (U)	
66139	aosk	WBAE	DBC	EWS	TO	
66140	aosk	WBAE	DBC	EWS	TO	
66142	aosk	WBAR	DBC	MRD	TO	Maritime Intermodal Three
66143	aosk	WQAA	DBC	EWS	TO (S)	
66144	aoskq	WBAR	DBC	EWS	TO	
66145	aosk	WQAB	DBC	EWS	TO (U)	
66147	aos	WBAE	DBC	EWS	TO	
66148	aosk	WBAE	DBC	EWS	TO	
66149	aosk	WBAE	DBC	DBC	TO	
66150	aosk	WBAE	DBC	DBC	TO	
66151	aosk	WBAE	DBC	EWS	TO	
66152	aosk	WBAE	DBC	DBS	TO	Derek Holmes Railway Operator
66154	aosk	WBAE	DBC	EWS	TO	
66155	aosk	WBAE	DBC	EWS	TO	
66156	aosk	WBAE	DBC	EWS	TO	
66158	aosk	WBAE	DBC	EWS	TO	
66160	aosk	WBAE	DBC	EWS	KM	
66161	aosk	WBAE	DBC	EWS	TO	
66162	aosk	WBAR	DBC	MRD	TO	Maritime Intermodal Five
66164	aosk	WBAE	DBC	EWS	TO	
66165	aosq	WBAR	DBC	DBC	TO	
66167	aosk	WBAE	DBC	DBC	TO	
66168	aoskq	WBRT	DBC	EWS	TO	
66169	aos	WBAR	DBC	EWS	TO	
66170	aosk	WBAE	DBC	EWS	TO	
66171	aosq	WBAR	DBC	EWS	TO	
66172	aos	WBAE	DBC	EWS	TO	PAUL MELLANY

66174	aosk	WBAE	DBC	EWS	TO	
66175	aoskq	WBAE	DBC	DBC	TO	
66176	aoskq	WBAR	DBC	EWS	TO	
66177	aos	WBAT	DBC	EWS	TO	
66181	aoskq	WBRT	DBC	EWS	TO	
66182	aosk	WQAB	DBC	DBC	TO (U)	
66183	aosk	WBAE	DBC	EWS	TO	
66185	aosk	WBRT	DBC	DBS	TO	*DP WORLD London Gateway*
66186	aos	WBAE	DBC	EWS	TO	
66187	aosk	WBAE	DBC	EWS	TO	
66188	aoskq	WBAR	DBC	EWS	TO	
66192	aoskq	WBAR	DBC	DBC	TO	
66194	aoskq	WBAR	DBC	EWS	TO	
66197	aosk	WBAE	DBC	EWS	TO	
66198	aoskq	WBAR	DBC	EWS	TO	
66199	aosk	WBAE	DBC	EWS	TO	
66200	aosk	WBAE	DBC	EWS	TO	
66206	aoskq	WBRT	DBC	DBC	TO	
66207	aosk	WBAE	DBC	EWS	TO	
66221	aos	WBRT	DBC	EWS	TO	
66230	aosk	WQAB	DBC	EWS	TO (U)	

66003-250 have swinghead couplers
66136 has YIWU-LONDON TRAIN branding
Note: All DB Cargo Class 66/67s in the WQAA pool are expected to move back to active pools

Class 66/3 – ordered by Fastline Freight

Details as per Class 66/0 except:

Years introduced:	2008
Engine Type:	GM 12N-710G3B-T2
Traction Motor type:	GM-EMD D43TRC
Fuel tank capacity:	1,145gal (5,150lit)

66301	aosr	XHIM	BEA	DRX	KM	*Kingmoor TMD*
66302	aosr	XHIM	BEA	DRX	KM	*Endeavour*
66303	aosr	XHIM	BEA	DRX	KM	
66304	aosr	XHIM	BEA	DRX	KM	
66305	aosr	XHIM	BEA	DRX	KM	

Class 66/4 – ordered by DRS

Details as per Class 66/3 except:
Years introduced: 2006-08

66413	aos	DFIN	MAQ	GWO	LD	*Lest We Forget*
66414	aos	DFIN	MAQ	FPH	LD	
66415	aos	DFIN	MAQ	GWD	LD	
66416	aos	DFIN	MAQ	FPH	LD	
66418	aos	DFIN	MAQ	FPH	LD	*PATRIOT – IN MEMORY OF FALLEN RAILWAY EMPLOYEES*
66419	aos	DFIN	MAQ	GWD	LD	
66420	aos	DFIN	MAQ	FPH	LD	
66421	aos	XHIM	MAQ	DRX	KM	*Gresty Bridge TMD*
66422	aos	XHIM	MAQ	DRX	KM	
66423	aos	XHIM	MAQ	DRX	KM	
66424	aos	XHIM	MAQ	DRX	KM	

66425	aos	XHIM	MAQ	DRX	KM	
66426	aos	XHIM	MAQ	DRX	KM	
66427	aos	XHIM	MAQ	DRX	KM	
66428	aos	XHIM	MAQ	DRX	KM	*Carlisle Eden Mind*
66429	aos	XHIM	MAQ	DRX	KM	
66430	aos	XHIM	MAQ	DRX	KM	
66431	aos	XHIM	MAQ	DRX	KM	
66432	aos	XHIM	MAQ	DRX	KM	
66433	aos	XHIM	MAQ	DRX	KM	
66434	aos	XHIM	MAQ	DRX	KM	

Class 66/5 – ordered by Freightliner

Details for 66501-572 as per Class 66/0, details for 66585-599 as per Class 66/3 except:
Years introduced: 1999-2008

66501	aos	DFIM	POR	FLR	LD	*Japan 2001*
66502	aos	DFIM	POR	FLR	LD	*Basford Hall Centenary 2001*
66503	aos	DFIM	POR	FLR	LD	*The RAILWAY MAGAZINE*
66504	aos	DFIM	POR	FPH	LD	
66505	aos	DFIM	POR	FLR	LD	
66506	aos	DFIM	EVS	FLR	LD	*Crewe Regeneration*
66507	aosc	DFIM	EVS	FLR	LD	
66508	aos	DFIM	EVS	FLR	LD	
66509	aos	DFIM	EVS	FLR	LD	
66510	aosc	DFIM	EVS	FLR	LD	
66511	aos	DFIM	EVS	FLR	LD	
66512	aos	DFIM	EVS	FLR	LD	
66513	aos	DFIM	EVS	FLR	LD	
66514	aos	DFIM	EVS	FLR	LD	
66515	aos	DFIM	EVS	FLR	LD	
66516	aos	DFIM	EVS	FLR	LD	
66517	aos	DFIM	EVS	FLR	LD	
66518	aos	DFIM	EVS	FLR	LD	
66519	aosc	DFIM	EVS	FLR	LD	
66520	aos	DFIM	EVS	FLR	LD	
66522	aosc	DFIM	EVS	FLR	LD	
66523	aos	DFIM	EVS	FLR	LD	
66524	aos	DFIM	EVS	FLR	LD	
66525	aos	DFIM	EVS	FLR	LD	
66526	aos	DFIM	EVS	FLR	LD	*Driver Steve Dunn (George)*
66528	aos	DFIM	POR	FPH	LD	*Madge Elliot MBE Borders Railway Opening 2015*
66529	aos	DFIM	POR	FLR	LD	
66531	aos	DFIM	POR	FLR	LD	
66532	aos	DFIM	POR	FLR	LD	*P&O Nedlloyd Atlas*
66533	aos	DFIM	POR	FLR	LD	*Hanjin Express/Senator Express*
66534	aos	DFIM	POR	FLR	LD	*OOCL Express*
66536	aos	DFIM	POR	FLR	LD	
66537	aos	DFIM	POR	FLR	LD	
66538	aos	DFIM	EVS	FLR	LD	
66539	aos	DFIM	EVS	FLR	LD	
66540	aos	DFIM	EVS	FLR	LD	*Ruby*
66541	aos	DFIM	EVS	FLR	LD	
66542	aos	DFIM	EVS	FLR	LD	
66543	aos	DFIM	EVS	FLR	LD	

66544	aos	DFIM	EVS	FLR	LD	
66545	aos	DFIM	POR	FLR	LD	
66546	aos	DFIM	POR	FLR	LD	
66547	aos	DFIM	POR	FLR	LD	
66548	aos	DFIM	POR	FLR	LD	
66549	aos	DFIM	POR	FLR	LD	
66550	aos	DFIM	POR	FLR	LD	
66551	aos	DFIM	POR	FLR	LD	
66552	aos	DFIM	POR	FLR	LD	*Maltby Raider*
66553	aos	DFIM	POR	FLR	LD	
66554	aos	DFIM	EVS	FLR	LD	
66555	aos	DFIM	EVS	FLR	LD	
66556	aos	DFIM	EVS	FLR	LD	
66557	aos	DFIM	EVS	FLR	LD	
66558	aos	DFIM	EVS	FLR	LD	
66559	aos	DFIM	EVS	FLR	LD	
66560	aos	DFIM	EVS	FLR	LD	
66561	aos	DFIM	EVS	FLR	LD	
66562	aos	DFIM	EVS	FLR	LD	
66563	aos	DFIM	EVS	FLR	LD	
66564	aos	DFIM	EVS	FLR	LD	
66565	aos	DFIM	EVS	FLR	LD	
66566	aos	DFIM	EVS	FLR	LD	
66567	aos	DFIM	EVS	FLR	LD	
66568	aos	DFIM	EVS	FLR	LD	
66569	aos	DFIM	EVS	FLR	LD	
66570	aos	DFIM	EVS	FLR	LD	
66571	aos	DFIM	EVS	FLR	LD	
66572	aos	DFIM	EVS	FLR	LD	
66585	aos	DFIN	MAQ	FLR	LD	
66587	aos	DFIN	MAQ	ONE	LD	*AS ONE, WE CAN*
66588	aos	DFIN	MAQ	FLR	LD	
66589	aos	DFIN	MAQ	FLR	LD	
66590	aos	DFIN	MAQ	FLR	LD	
66591	aos	DFIN	MAQ	FLR	LD	
66592	aos	DFIN	MAQ	FLR	LD	*Johnson Stevens Agencies*
66593	aos	DFIN	MAQ	FLR	LD	*3MG MERSEY MULTIMODAL GATEWAY*
66594	aos	DFIN	MAQ	FLR	LD	*NYK Spirit of Kyoto*
66596	aos	DFIN	BEA	FLR	LD	
66597	aos	DFIN	BEA	FLR	LD	*Viridor*
66598	aos	DFIN	BEA	FLR	LD	
66599	aos	DFIN	BEA	FLR	LD	

Class 66/6 – regeared locos ordered by Freightliner

Details for 66601-622 as per Class 66/0, details for 66623 as per Class 66/3 except:

Years introduced:	2000-07
Maximum tractive effort:	105,080lbf (467kN)
Continuous tractive effort:	66,630lbf (296kN)
Maximum design speed:	65mph (104km/h)

66601	aos	DFHH	POR	FLR	LD	*The Hope Valley*
66602	aos	DFHH	POR	FLR	LD	
66603	aos	DFHH	POR	FLR	LD	
66604	aos	DFHH	POR	FLR	LD	
66605	aos	DFHH	POR	FLR	LD	
66606	aos	DFHH	POR	FLR	LD	

66607	aos	DFHH	POR	FLR	LD	
66610	aos	DFHH	POR	FLR	LD	
66613	aos	DFHH	EVS	FLR	LD	
66614	aos	DFHH	EVS	FLR	LD	*1916 POPPY 2016*
66615	aos	DFHH	EVS	FLR	LD	
66616	aos	DFHH	EVS	FLR	LD	
66617	aos	DFHH	EVS	FLR	LD	
66618	aos	DFHH	EVS	FLR	LD	*Railways Illustrated Annual Photographic Awards Alan Barnes*
66619	aos	DFHH	EVS	FLR	LD	*Derek W. Johnson MBE*
66620	aos	DFHH	EVS	FLR	LD	
66621	aos	DFHH	EVS	FLR	LD	
66622	aos	DFHH	EVS	FLR	LD	
66623	aos	DFHH	MAQ	GWD	LD	

Class 66/7 – locos ordered or acquired by GB Railfreight

Details for 66701-751 as per Class 66/0, details for 66752-779 as per Class 66/3 except:

Years introduced:	2001-16
Engine:	EMD 12N-710G3B-T2 (66718-732/747-749)
Traction Motor type:	GM-EMD D43TRC (66718-732/747-749)
Fuel tank capacity:	1,440gal (6,550lit) 66701-717/733-746/750/751, 1,220gal (5,546lit) – 66718-722, 1,312gal (5,150lit) – 66723-732/747-749/752-779

66701	aos	GBBT	EVS	GBO	RR	
66702	aos	GBBT	EVS	GBR	RR	*Blue Lightning*
66703	aos	GBBT	EVS	GBR	RR	*Doncaster PSB 1981-2002*
66704	aos	GBBT	EVS	GBR	RR	*Colchester Power Signalbox*
66705	aos	GBBT	EVS	GBR	RR	*Golden Jubilee*
66706	aos	GBBT	EVS	GBR	RR	*Nene Valley*
66707	aos	GBBT	EVS	GBR	RR	*Sir Sam Fay*
66708	aos	GBBT	EVS	GBR	RR	*Jayne*
66709	aos	GBBT	EVS	MSC	RR	*Sorrento*
66710	aos	GBBT	EVS	GBR	RR	*Phil Packer BRIT*
66711	aos	GBBT	EVS	AGI	RR	*Sence*
66712	aos	GBBT	EVS	GBR	RR	*Peterborough Power Signalbox*
66713	aos	GBBT	EVS	GBR	RR	*Forest City*
66714	aos	GBBT	EVS	GBR	RR	*Cromer Lifeboats*
66715	aos	GBBT	EVS	GBR	RR	*VALOUR*
66716	aos	GBBT	EVS	GBR	RR	*LOCOMOTIVE & CARRIAGE INSTITUTION CENTENARY 1911-2011*
66717	aos	GBBT	EVS	GBR	RR	*Good Old Boy*
66718	aos	GBLT	EVS	LUB	RR	*Sir Peter Hendy CBE*
66719	aos	GBLT	EVS	GBR	RR	*METRO-LAND*
66720	aos	GBLT	EVS	EMY	RR	
66721	aos	GBLT	EVS	LUW	RR	*Harry Beck*
66722	aos	GBLT	EVS	GBR	RR	*Sir Edward Watkin*
66723	aos	GBLT	EVS	GBZ	RR	*Chinook*
66724	aos	GBLT	EVS	GBF	RR	*Drax Power Station*
66725	aos	GBLT	EVS	GBZ	RR	*SUNDERLAND*
66726	aos	GBLT	EVS	GBF	RR	*SHEFFIELD WEDNESDAY*
66727	aos	GBLT	EVS	MRT	RR	*Maritime One*
66728	aos	GBLT	EVS	GBR	RR	*Institution of Railway Operators*

66729		aos	GBLT	EVS	GBR	RR	*DERBY COUNTY*
66730		aos	GBLT	EVS	GBR	RR	*Whitemoor*
66731		aos	GBLT	EVS	GBR	RR	*InterhubGB*
66732		aos	GBLT	EVS	GBR	RR	*GBRF The First Decade 1999-2009 John Smith MD*
66733	66401	aosr	GBFM	POR	GBR	RR	*Cambridge PSB*
66735	66403	aosr	GBBT	POR	GBR	RR	*PETERBOROUGH UNITED*
66736	66404	aosr	GBFM	POR	GBR	RR	*WOLVERHAMPTON WANDERERS*
66737	66405	aosr	GBFM	POR	GBR	RR	*Lesia*
66738	66578	aosr	GBBT	BEA	GBR	RR	*HUDDERSFIELD TOWN*
66739	66579	aos	GBFM	BEA	GBR	RR	*Bluebell Railway*
66740	66580	aosr	GBFM	BEA	GBR	RR	*Sarah*
66741	66581	aos	GBBT	BEA	GBR	RR	*Swanage Railway*
66742	66406, 66841	aos	GBBT	BEA	GBR	RR	*ABP Port of Immingham Centenary 1912-2012*
66743	66407, 66842	aosr	GBFM	BEA	ROY	RR	
66744	66408, 66843	aos	GBBT	BEA	GBR	RR	*Crossrail*
66745	66409, 66844	aos	GBRT	BEA	GBR	RR	*Modern Railways The first 50 years*
66746	66410, 66845	aostr	GBFM	BEA	ROY	RR	
66747		aos	GBEB	GBR	NWT	RR	*Made in Sheffield*
66748		aos	GBEB	GBR	GBR	RR	*West Burton 50*
66749		aos	GBEB	GBR	GBR	RR	
66750		aos	GBEB	BEA	GBR	RR	*Bristol Panel Signal Box*
66751		aos	GBEB	BEA	GBR	RR	*Inspirational Delivered Hitachi Rail Europe*
66752		aos	GBEL	GBR	GBR	RR	*The Hoosier State*
66753		aos	GBEL	GBR	GBR	RR	*EMD Roberts Road*
66754		aos	GBEL	GBR	GBR	RR	*Northampton Saints*
66755		aos	GBEL	GBR	GBR	RR	*Tony Berkeley OBE RFG Chairman 1997-2018*
66756		aos	GBEL	GBR	GBR	RR	*Royal Corps of Signals*
66757		aos	GBEL	GBR	GBR	RR	*West Somerset Railway*
66758		aos	GBEL	GBR	GBR	RR	*The Pavior*
66759		aos	GBEL	GBR	GBR	RR	*Chippy*
66760		aos	GBEL	GBR	GBR	RR	*David Gordon Harris*
66761		aos	GBEL	GBR	GBR	RR	*Wensleydale Railway Association 25 Years 1990-2015*
66762		aos	GBEL	GBR	GBR	RR	
66763		aos	GBEL	GBR	GBR	RR	*Severn Valley Railway*
66764		aos	GBEL	GBR	GBR	RR	
66765		aos	GBEL	GBR	GBR	RR	
66766		aos	GBEL	GBR	GBR	RR	
66767		aos	GBEL	GBR	GBR	RR	
66768		aos	GBEL	GBR	GBR	RR	
66769		aos	GBEL	GBR	GBR	RR	
66770		aos	GBEL	GBR	GBR	RR	
66771		aos	GBEL	GBR	GBR	RR	*Amanda*
66772		aos	GBEL	GBR	GBR	RR	*Maria*
66773		aos	GBNB	GBR	GBP	RR	*Pride in GB Railfreight*
66774		aos	GBNB	GBR	GBR	RR	
66775		aos	GBNB	GBR	GBZ	RR	*HMS Argyll*
66776		aos	GBNB	GBR	GBR	RR	*Joanne*
66777		aos	GBNB	GBR	GBR	RR	*Annette*
66778		aos	GBNB	GBR	GBR	RR	*Cambois Depot 25 Years*
66779		aos	GBEL	GBR	GYP	RR	*EVENING STAR*
66780	66008	aos	GBOB	GBR	CMX	RR	*The Cemex Express*

66781	66016	aos	GBOB	GBR	GBR	RR	
66782	66046	aos	GBOB	GBR	GBZ	RR	
66783	66058	aos	GBOB	GBR	BIF	RR	*The Flying Dustman*
66784	66081	aos	GBOB	GBR	GBR	RR	*Keighley & Worth Valley Railway 50th Anniversary 1968-2018*
66785	66132	aos	GBOB	GBR	GBR	RR	
66786	66141	aos	GBOB	GBR	GBR	RR	
66787	66184	aos	GBOB	GBR	GBR	RR	
66788	66238	aos	GBOB	GBR	GBR	RR	*LOCOMOTION 15*
66789	66250	aos	GBOB	GBR	BLL	RR	*British Rail 1948-1997*
66790	CD66403	aos	MBDL	BEA	BLU	ZW (U)	
66791	CD66404	aos	MBDL	BEA	BLU	ZW (U)	
66792	CD66405	aos	MBDL	BEA	RRB	ZW (U)	

Note: 66723 carries ZA723 as well as its TOPS number
Note: 66775 carries F231 as well as its TOPS number

Class 66/8 – locos acquired by Colas Rail Freight

Details as per Class 66/0 except:
| Years introduced: | 2003/04 (as 66/5s) |
| Fuel tank capacity: | 1,440gal (6,550lit) |

66846	66573	aost	COLO	BEA	COL	RU	
66847	66574	aost	COLO	BEA	COL	RU	*Terry Baker*
66848	66575	aost	COLO	BEA	COL	RU	
66849	66576	aost	COLO	BEA	COL	RU	*Wylam Dilly*
66850	66577	aost	COLO	BEA	COL	RU	*David Maidment OBE*

Class 66/9 – low emission locos ordered by Freightliner

Details as per Class 66/3 except:
| Years introduced: | 2004/08 |
| Fuel tank capacity: | 1,224gal (5,510lit); t – 1,312gal (5,905lit) |

66951		aost	DFIN	EVS	FLR	LD	
66952		aos	DFIN	EVS	FLR	LD	
66953		aos	DFIN	BEA	FLR	LD	
66955		aos	DFIN	BEA	FLR	LD	
66956		aos	DFIN	BEA	FLR	LD	
66957		aos	DFIN	BEA	FLR	LD	*Stephenson Locomotive Society 1909-2009*

Euro Class 66s

These locos are European Spec Class 66s brought to the UK for repairs at Longport. They are added to TOPS to allow them to be moved on Network Rail infrastructure. They return the Netherlands once repairs are completed, but are included in this book as they have been hauled on NR infrastructure. Other Class 66s from Europe are expected to visit Longport and these may be added to TOPS.

66997	PB15	aos	GROC			HQ	*LOCO NOW RETURNED TO THE NETHERLANDS*
66998	PB13	aos	GROC			HQ	*LOCO NOW RETURNED TO THE NETHERLANDS*
66999	6601	aos	GROC			HQ	*LOCO NOW RETURNED TO THE NETHERLANDS*

Sporting its unique bright pink livery, 66587 *As One, We Can* works a container train from Southampton to Birmingham Lawley Street past Tyseley on 21 June 2019. *Ian Nightingale*

No. 66955 heads north away from Spalding with the 1546 Felixstowe-Doncaster Europorte Freightliner Intermodal train on 28 May 2018. *Pip Dunn*

DB Cargo's 67010 drags LNER's 91125 on 1E06, the 0648 Glasgow Central-Kings Cross, past the Metro Centre on the Carlisle-Newcastle line on 29 September 2018. *Anthony Hicks*

Class 67

Essentially a Bo-Bo, ETH fitted 125mph mixed traffic version of the Class 66, 30 locos were ordered by EWS and delivered in 1999-2000. Two have since been sold to Colas Rail Freight, but reducing work means several are withdrawn.

Built by:	Alstom/General Motors, Valencia, Spain
Years introduced:	1999-2000
Wheel arrangement:	Bo-Bo
Weight:	90 tons
Length:	64ft 7in (19.71m)
Engine Type:	GM 12N-710G3B-EC
Engine output:	2,980hp (2,223kW)
Power at rail:	2,493hp (1,860kW)
Maximum tractive effort:	31,750lbf (141kN)
Continuous tractive effort:	20,200lbf (90kN)
ETH index:	66
Maximum design speed:	125mph (200km/h) restricted to 110mph (177km/h)
Brake Force:	78 tons
Route Availability:	8
Traction alternator:	GM-EMD AR9A
Companion alternator:	GM-EMD CA6HEX
Traction Motor type:	GM-EMD D43FM
Fuel tank capacity	1,095gal (4,927lit)
Multiple Working type:	AAR

67001	aep	WAAC	DBC	ATW	CE	
67002	aep	WAAC	DBC	ATW	CE	
67003	aep	WQAA	DBC	ATW	TO (S)	
67004	aepr	WABC	DBC	DBC	CE	
67005	aep	WAAC	DBC	RTO	CE	Queen's Messenger
67006	aep	WAAC	DBC	RTO	CE	Royal Sovereign
67007	aepr	WQAA	DBC	EWS	TO (S)	
67008	aep	WACC	DBC	EWS	CE	
67009	aepr	WQBA	DBC	EWS	CE (U)	
67010	aep	WAWC	DBC	DBC	CE	
67011	aepr	WQBA	DBC	EWS	CE (U)	
67012	aep	WAWC	DBC	CRS	CE	
67013	aep	WAAC	DBC	DBC	CE	
67014	aep	WAWC	DBC	CRS	CE	
67015	aep	WAAC	DBC	CRS	CE	
67016	aep	WAAC	DBC	EWS	CE	
67017	aep	WQAA	DBC	EWS	CE (S)	Arrow
67018	aep	WQAA	DBC	DBS	CE (S)	Keith Heller
67019	aep	WQBA	DBC	EWS	TO (U)	
67020	aep	WAAC	DBC	EWS	CE	
67021	aep	WAAC	DBC	PUL	CE	
67022	aep	WQAA	DBC	EWS	CE (S)	
67023	aep	COTS	BEA	COL	RU	Charlotte
67024	aep	WAAC	DBC	PUL	CE	
67025	aep	WQAA	DBC	TFW	TO (S)	Western Star
67026	aep	WQBA	DBC	JUB	CE (U)	Diamond Jubilee
67027	aep	COTS	BEA	COL	RU	Stella
67028	aep	WAAC	DBC	DBC	CE	
67029	aepq	WACC	DBC	DBM	CE	Royal Diamond
67030	aepr	WQAA	DBC	EWS	TO (S)	

67010 has 'First choice for rail freight in the UK' branding
67028 has 'Leading the next generation of rail freight' branding
67001-030 have swinghead couplers

Class 68

New mixed traffic Bo-Bo loco ordered by DRS in 2012. Initial order for 15 upped to 25, then 32 and presently 34 locos. More could be ordered. Nos 68019-032 are dedicated for Transpennine use and 68010-015 are dedicated to Chiltern Railways services.

Built by:	Vossloh/Stadler, Valencia
Years introduced:	2014-17
Wheel arrangement:	Bo-Bo
Weight:	85 tons
Length:	20.5m
Engine Type:	Caterpillar C175-16
Engine output:	3,805hp (2,839kW)
Power at rail:	3,190hp (2,380kW)
Tractive effort:	71,260lbf (317kN)
Continuous tractive effort	56,200lbf (250kN)
ETH index:	96
Maximum design speed:	100mph (160km/h)
Brake Force:	73 tons
Route Availability:	7
Main alternator type:	ABB WGX560
Traction Motor type:	ABB 4FRA6063

Fuel tank capacity: 1,120gal (5,600lit)
Multiple Working type: within class and Class 88 only

68001	aep*	XHVE	BEA	DRN	CR	*Evolution*
68002	aep*	XHVE	BEA	DRN	CR	*Intrepid*
68003	aep*	XHVE	BEA	DRN	CR	*Astute*
68004	aep*	XHVE	BEA	DRN	CR	*Rapid*
68005	aep*	XHVE	BEA	DRN	CR	*Defiant*
68006	aep*	XHVE	BEA	SCR	CR	*Daring*
68007	aep*	XHVE	BEA	SCR	CR	*Valiant*
68008	aeup*	XHVE	BEA	DRN	CR	*Avenger*
68009	aeup*	XHVE	BEA	DRN	CR	*Titan*
68010	aeup*	XHCE	BEA	CRS	CR	*Oxford Flyer*
68011	aeup*	XHCE	BEA	CRS	CR	
68012	aeup*	XHCE	BEA	CRS	CR	
68013	aeup*	XHCE	BEA	CRS	CR	
68014	aeup*	XHCE	BEA	CRS	CR	
68015	aeup*	XHCE	BEA	CRS	CR	
68016	aep*	XHVE	BEA	DRN	CR	*Fearless*
68017	aep*	XHVE	BEA	DRN	CR	*Hornet*
68018	aep*	XHVE	BEA	DRN	CR	*Vigilant*
68019	aeup*	TPEX	BEA	TPE	CR	*Brutus*
68020	aeup*	TPEX	BEA	TPE	CR	*Reliance*
68021	aeup*	XHTP	BEA	TPE	CR	*Tireless*
68022	aeup*	TPEX	BEA	TPE	CR	*Resolution*
68023	aeup*	TPEX	BEA	TPE	CR	*Achilles*
68024	aeup*	TPEX	BEA	TPE	CR	*Centaur*
68025	aeup*	XHTP	BEA	TPE	CR	*Superb*

One of two DRS Class 68s in ScotRail's Saltire livery, 68007 *Valiant* heads 2K01, the 0635 Edinburgh-Glenrothes with Thornton, past Burntisland on 10 May 2019. *Anthony Hicks*

68026		aep*	XHTP	BEA	TPE	CR	*Enterprise*
68027		aep*	TPEX	BEA	TPE	CR	*Splendid*
68028		aep*	TPEX	BEA	TPE	CR	*Lord President*
68029		aep*	TPEX	BEA	TPE	CR	*Courageous*
68030		aep*	XHTP	BEA	TPE	CR	*Black Douglas*
68031		aep*	TPEX	BEA	TPE	CR	*Felix*
68032		aep*	XHTP	BEA	TPE	CR	*Destroyer*
68033		aep*	XHVE	DRS	DRN	CR	
68034		aep*	XHVE	DRS	DRN	CR	

Note: XHVE/XHCE and XHTP locos have different push-pull systems and are not interoperable between the pools

Class 69

These locomotives are Class 56s being rebuilt with the same engines as used in Class 66s. They are for use with GB Railfreight. Technical details may change. The first loco is expected to be ready for testing in early 2020. The number of locos expected to be rebuilt is likely to be between 10 and 17.

Built by:	Progress Rail, Longport Stoke
Years introduced:	2019-21
Wheel arrangement:	Co-Co
Weight:	126 tons
Length:	63ft 6in (19.39m)
Engine Type:	GM 12N-710G3B-EC
Engine output:	3,300hp (2,462kW)
Power at rail:	3,000hp (2,238kW)
Maximum tractive effort:	92,000lbf (409kN)
Continuous tractive effort:	58,390lbf (260kN)
Maximum design speed:	75mph (120km/h)
Brake Force:	60 tons
Route Availability:	7
Traction alternator:	GM-EMD AR8
Companion alternator:	GM-EMD CA6
Traction Motor type:	GM-EMD D43TR
Fuel tank capacity:	1,150gal (5,228lit)
Multiple Working type:	AAR

69001	56057, 56311	aos	GBR
69002		aos	GBR
69003		aos	GBR
69004		aos	GBR
69005		aos	GBR
69006		aos	GBR
69007		aos	GBR
69008		aos	GBR
69009		aos	GBR
69010		aos	GBR
69011		aos	GBR
69012		aos	GBR
69013		aos	GBR
69014		aos	GBR
69015		aos	GBR
69016		aos	GBR
69017		aos	GBR

Class 70

General Electric freight loco design ordered by Freightliner. The initial order was for 20 locos with an option for ten more, which was not taken up. Instead those locos were taken by Colas Rail Freight, which later ordered seven more.

Freightliner's 70012 was delivered to the UK but badly damaged when it was dropped by the crane during unloading, so it was returned to the USA and is deemed as disposed. No. 70801 was formerly a demonstrator loco numbered 70099 that was built from a kit delivered to Turkey and shipped to the UK before being taken on by Colas. Several Freightliner locos have been stood down in recent times due to poor reliability and changing traffic patterns.

Built by:	General Electric, Erie, Pennsylvania
Years introduced:	2009-12
Wheel arrangement:	Co-Co
Weight:	129 tons
Length:	21.71m
Engine Type:	GE Powerhaul P616LDA1
Engine output:	3,820hp (2,848kW)
Power at rail:	2,700hp (2,014kW)
Tractive effort:	122,000lbf (544kN)
Continuous tractive effort	96,000lbf (427kN)
Maximum design speed:	75mph (120km/h)
Brake Force:	96.7 tons
Route Availability:	7
Main alternator type:	GE 5GTAZ6721A1
Traction Motor type:	AC-GE 5GEB30B
Fuel tank capacity:	1,333gal (6,000lit)
Multiple Working type:	AAR

Class 70/0 – Freightliner Locos

70001		aos	DFGI	MAQ	FPH	LD	PowerHaul
70002		aos	DFGI	MAQ	FPH	LD	
70003		aos	DFGI	MAQ	FPH	LD	
70004		aos	DHLT	MAQ	FPH	LD (U)	The Coal Industry Society
70005		aos	DFGI	MAQ	FPH	LD	
70006		aos	DFGI	MAQ	FPH	LD	
70007		aos	DFGI	MAQ	FPH	LD	
70008		aos	DFGI	MAQ	FPH	LD	
70009		aos	DHLT	MAQ	FPH	LD (U)	
70010		aos	DFGI	MAQ	FPH	LD	
70011		aos	DHLT	MAQ	FPH	LD (S)	
70013		aos	DHLT	MAQ	FPH	LD (U)	
70014		aos	DHLT	MAQ	FPH	LD (S)	
70015		aos	DFGI	MAQ	FPH	LD	
70016		aos	DHLT	MAQ	FPH	LD (U)	
70017		aos	DHLT	MAQ	FPH	LD (U)	
70018		aos	DHLT	MAQ	FPH	LD (U)	
70019		aos	DHLT	MAQ	FPH	LD (U)	
70020		aos	DFGI	MAQ	FPH	LD	

Class 70/8 – Colas Rail Freight locos
Details as per Class 70/0

70801	70099	aos	COLO	BEA	COL	CF

Freightliner's 70006 passes Basingstoke with 4O14, the 0536 Garston-Southampton Maritime on 10 April 2019. Most Freightliner Class 70s are currently stored. *Mark Pike*

Colas has 17 Class 70s in its fleet. One of the second batch of seven locos, 70813 passes Glass's Crossing at Bathampton with 6C37, 1628 Westbury-Aberthaw empty cement tanks on 1 September 2017. *Glen Batten*

70802	aos	COLO	BEA	COL	CF
70803	aos	COLO	BEA	COL	CF
70804	aos	COLO	BEA	COL	CF
70805	aos	COLO	BEA	COL	CF
70806	aos	COLO	BEA	COL	CF
70807	aos	COLO	BEA	COL	CF
70808	aos	COLO	BEA	COL	CF
70809	aos	COLO	BEA	COL	CF
70810	aos	COLO	BEA	COL	CF
70811	aos	COLO	BEA	COL	CF
70812	aos	COLO	BEA	COL	CF
70813	aos	COLO	BEA	COL	CF
70814	aos	COLO	BEA	COL	CF
70815	aos	COLO	BEA	COL	CF
70816	aos	COLO	BEA	COL	CF
70817	aos	COLO	BEA	COL	CF

Class 73

A fleet of six prototype Electro Diesel locos (Class 73/0) was built in 1962 by BR at Eastleigh followed by a production series of 43 locos (Class 73/1) built by EE at Vulcan Foundry in 1965. In 1988, 12, later increased to 14, locos were modified for dedicated Gatwick Express use (Class 73/2) while two 73/0s were converted for Sandite use on Merseyrail as Class 73/9s. Two re-engineering programmes have been undertaken, one by RVEL (now LORAM) at Derby for Network Rail that saw the EE diesel engine replaced by two Cummins engines. Only two locos have been modified and no more conversions are expected. Brush also rebuilt 11 locos for GBRf with single MTU engines. Five of these are for NR contacts (73961-965) while the other six (73966-971) are dedicated for Caledonian Sleeper work in Scotland. There are a few differences between these two fleets. More GBRf conversions may be forthcoming and the company still retains a sizeable fleet of original 73s still in main line use, recently adding further locos to its spares pool.

Built by:	English Electric, Vulcan Foundry
Years introduced:	1962-67
Wheel arrangement:	Bo-Bo
Weight:	76-77 tons
Length:	53ft 8in (16.96m)
Power supply:	750V DC third rail
Engine Type:	English Electric 4SRKT Mk 2
Engine output:	600hp (447kW)
Electric output:	1,600hp (1,193kW)
Power at rail (diesel):	402hp (300kW)
Electric power at rail (Cont):	1,200hp (895kW)
Electric power at rail (Max):	2,450hp (1,830kW)
Electric tractive effort:	40,000lb (179kN) – Electric
Diesel tractive effort:	36,000lbf (160kN) – Diesel
Continuous tractive effort	13,600lbf (60kN) – Diesel
ETH index:	38 on electric power only
Maximum design speed:	90mph (144km/h)
Brake Force:	31 tons
Route Availability:	6
Main generator type:	EE824-3D
Auxiliary generator type:	EE908-3C
Traction Motor type:	EE546-1B

| Fuel tank capacity: | 310gal (1,409lit) |
| Multiple Working type: | Blue Star |

Class 73/0: original build locos

| 73001 | E6001, 73901 | xew | MBED | LSL | BRB | CD (S) |
| 73002 | E6002 | xew | MBED | LSL | LLB | ZG (U) |

Class 73/1: standard locos

73101	E6007, 73801	xew	GBSD	GBR	PUL	ZG (U)	
73107	E6013	xew	GBED	GBR	GBR	SE	Tracy
73109	E6015	xew	GBED	GBR	GBR	SE	
73110	E6016	xew		GBR	EBY	ZG (U)	
73119	E6025	xew	GBED	GBR	GBR	SE	Borough of Eastleigh
73128	E6035	xew	GBED	GBR	GBR	SE	OVS BULLEID CBE
73134	E6041	xew	GBBR	GBR	ICO	BL (U)	
73136	E6043	xew	GBED	GBR	GBR	SE	Mhairi
73138	E6045	aew	QADD	NET	NRY	SE	
73139	E6046	xew	GBSD	GBR	UND	ZG (U)	
73141	E6048	xew	GBED	GBR	GBR	SE	Charlotte
73201	E6049, 73142	aew	GBED	GBR	BRB	SE	Broadlands
73202	E6044, 73137	aew	MBED	POR	SOU	SL	Graham Stenning
73212	E6008, 73102	aewp*	GBED	GBR	GBR	SE	Fiona
73213	E6018, 73112	aewp*	GBED	GBR	GBR	SE	Rhodalyn
73235	E6042, 73135	aew	HYWD	POR	SWU	BM	

Note: 73212/213 have snowplough brackets at one end only

Class 73/9 – LORAM rebuilt locos
Details as per Class 73/1 except:
| Built by: | LORAM |
| Years introduced: | 2015 |

Network Rail's Cummins-powered 73952 *Janis Kong* and 73951 *Malcolm Brinded* pass Woking arriving light from Derby RTC on 15 June 2017. *Mark Pike*

Engine type	two Cummins QSK19
Engine output (total):	1,500hp (1,119kW)
Power at rail (diesel):	1,005hp (750kW)
Electric tractive effort:	40,000lbf (179kN)
Diesel tractive effort:	40,000lbf (179kN)
Maximum design speed:	90mph
Brake Force:	31 tonnes
Fuel tank capacity:	500gal (2,260lit)
Multiple Working type:	AAR

73951	E6010, 73104	ao	QADD	NET	NRY	ZA		*Malcolm Brinded*
73952	E6019, 73113, 73211	ao	QADD	NET	NRY	ZA		*Janis Kong*

Class 73/9 – Brush rebuilt locos

Details as per Class 73/1 except:

Built by:	Brush Loughborough
Years introduced:	2014-15
Engine type	MTU R4000L 8V43
Engine output:	1,600hp (1,194kW)
Power at rail (diesel):	1,072hp (800kW)
ETH index:	50 (73961-965), 90 (73966-971)
Maximum design speed:	90mph

GB Railfreight's 73969, one of six locos dedicated to Caledonian Sleeper work, passes Clachnaharry with 0Z73, the 0930 Dingwall-Inverness on 3 July 2018. Visits by Class 73s north of Inverness are rare. *Graeme Elgar*

Brake Force:	31 tonnes
Main alternator type:	Lechmotoren SDV 87.53-12
Multiple Working type:	Blue Star and AAR

73961	E6026, 73120, 73209	aetwp	GBNR	GBR	GBR	SE	*Alison*
73962	E6032, 73125, 73204	aetwp	GBNR	GBR	GBR	SE	*Dick Mabbutt*
73963	E6030, 73123, 73206	aetwp	GBNR	GBR	GBR	SE	*Janice*
73964	E6031, 73124, 73205	aetwp	GBNR	GBR	GBR	SE	*Jeanette*
73965	E6028, 73121, 73208	aetwp	GBNR	GBR	GBR	SE	
73966	E6005, 73005	aetrdp*	GBCS	GBR	CAL	EC	
73967	E6006, 73006, 73906	aetrdp*	GBCS	GBR	CAL	EC	
73968	E6023, 73117	aetrdp*	GBCS	GBR	CAL	EC	
73969	E6011, 73105	aetrdp*	GBCS	GBR	CAL	EC	
73970	E6009, 73103	aetrdp*	GBCS	GBR	CAL	EC	
73971	E6029, 73122, 73207	aetrdp*	GBCS	GBR	CAL	EC	

Note: 73962/964 have cab end brackets for fitting ladders for working on the East London Line
The 750V DC capability on 73966-971 is currently isolated

Class 86

The standard 25kV AC loco built for BR in the mid-1960s, totalling 100 examples. Sixty-one were modified to Class 86/2s, while the remaining Class 86/0s were later changed to either Class 86/3s or 86/4s, with the 86/3s duly becoming 86/4s. Of the 39 Class 86/4s, 30 were converted to freight only Class 86/6s, 16 of which remain in traffic with Freightliner. These are expected to be phased out in 2020 when Class 90s become available from Greater Anglia. Nos 86101/401 have been on hire to GBRf but this contract is expected to end soon. Several Class 86/2s have been exported for use in Bulgaria and Hungary.

Built by:	English Electric Vulcan Foundry and BR Doncaster
Years introduced:	1965-66
Wheel arrangement:	Bo-Bo
Weight:	83-87 tons
Length:	58ft 6in (17.83m)
Power supply:	25kV AC
Control system:	HT tap changing
Traction output (max):	7,680hp (5,860kW)
Traction output (cont.):	5,000hp (3,730kW)
Tractive effort:	58,000lb (258kN)
ETH index:	74
Maximum design speed:	100-110mph (160-180km/h)
Brake Force:	40 tons
Route Availability:	6
Traction Motor type:	GEC G412AZ
Multiple Working type:	TDM

Class 86/1 – test locos

86101	E3191, 86201	xe		GBCH	ACL	CAL	WN	*Sir William A Stanier FRS*

Class 86/2 – standard locos

Details as per Class 86/1 except:
Traction output (max):	6,100hp (4,550kW)
Traction output (cont.):	4,040hp (3,013kW)
Traction Motor type:	AEI 282AZ

86259	E3137, 86045	xe	MBEL	LES	EBY	WN	*Les Ross/Peter Pan*

Class 86/4 – regeared locos

Details as per Class 86/1 except:
Traction output (max):	5,900hp (4,400kW)
Traction output (cont.):	3,600hp (2,680kW)
Traction Motor type:	AEI 282AZ

86401	E3199, 86001	xe	GBCH	ACL	CAL	WN	*Mons Meg*

Class 86/6 – freight only locos

Details as per Class 86/1 except:
Traction output (max):	5,900hp (4,400kW)
Traction output (cont.):	3,600hp (2,680kW)
Maximum design speed:	75mph (120km/h)
Traction Motor type:	AEI 282AZ
No train heating	

Two of Freightliner Intermodal's Class 86s, 86638 and 86628 emerge from Ipswich Tunnel with 4L41, 0604 Crewe Basford Hall-Felixstowe on 25 April 2019. These locos are expected to be retired very soon and replaced by Class 90s. *Glen Batten*

86604	E3103, 86004, 86404	aym	DFNC	FLI	FLH	CB
86605	E3185, 86005, 86405	aym	DFNC	FLI	FLH	CB
86607	E3176, 86007, 86407	aym	DFNC	FLI	FLH	CB
86608	E3180, 86008, 86408, 86501	aym	DFNC	FLI	FLH	CB
86609	E3102, 86009, 86409	aym	DFNC	FLI	FLH	CB
86610	E3104, 86010, 86410	aym	DFNC	FLI	FLH	CB
86612	E3122, 86012, 86312, 86412	aym	DFNC	POR	FLH	CB
86613	E3128, 86013, 86313, 86413	aym	DFNC	POR	FLH	CB
86614	E3145, 86014, 86314, 86414	aym	DFNC	POR	FLH	CB
86622	E3174, 86022, 86322, 86422	aym	DFNC	POR	FPH	CB
86627	E3110, 86027, 86327, 86427	aym	DFNC	POR	FLH	CB
86628	E3159, 86028, 86328, 86428	aym	DFNC	POR	FLH	CB
86632	E3148, 86032, 86432	aym	DFNC	POR	FLH	CB
86637	E3130, 86037, 86437	aym	DFNC	POR	FPH	CB
86638	E3108, 86038, 86438	aym	DFNC	POR	FLH	CB
86639	E3153, 86039, 86439	aym	DFNC	POR	FLH	CB

On 29 September 2018, privately owned 86259 *Les Ross* waits at Carlisle to work a WCR charter back to London. *Robin Ralston*

Class 87

An improved version of the Class 86, 36 locos were built from 1973 for the newly electrified northern section of the WCML. The last of the class were withdrawn by Virgin Trains in the early 2000s. Several have been exported to Bulgaria. One loco remains UK main line registered, on spot hire to GBRf but could be returned to its owners soon.

Built by:	BREL Crewe
Years introduced:	1973-74
Wheel arrangement:	Bo-Bo
Weight:	83 tons
Length:	58ft 6in (17.83m)
Power supply:	25kV AC
Control system:	HT tap changing
Traction output (max)	7,680hp (5,860kW)
Traction output (Con):	5,000hp (3,730kW)
Tractive effort:	58,000lb
ETH index:	95
Maximum design speed:	110mph (176km/h)
Brake Force:	40 tons
Route Availability:	6
Traction Motor type:	GEC G412AZ
Multiple Working type:	TDM

87002	ae	GBCH	ACL	CAL	WN	*Royal Sovereign*

Class 88 Electro Diesel

An Electro Diesel version of the Class 68 ordered for DRS. They are used mostly for intermodal trains on the West Coast Main Line.

Built by:	Vossloh/Stadler, Valencia
Years introduced:	2015
Wheel arrangement:	Bo-Bo
Weight:	85 tons
Length:	20.5m
Power supply:	25kV AC
Engine Type:	Caterpillar C27 12-cylinder
Engine output:	950hp (708kW)
Traction output (Con):	5,360hp (4,000kW)
Tractive effort:	71,260lbf (317kN)
ETH index:	96
Maximum design speed:	100mph (160km/h)
Brake Force:	88 tons
Route Availability:	7
Main alternator type:	ABB AMXL400
Traction Motor type:	ABB AMXL400
Fuel tank capacity:	400gal (1,800lit)
Multiple Working type:	Within Class and Class 68 only

88001	aeup*	XHVE	BEA	DRE	CR	*Revolution*
88002	aeup*	XHVE	BEA	DRE	CR	*Prometheus*
88003	aeup*	XHVE	BEA	DRE	CR	*Genesis*
88004	aeup*	XHVE	BEA	DRE	CR	*Pandora*

DRS's 88007 *Electra*, with dead 88004 *Pandora* on the rear, hauls the 6M50 Torness-Carlisle nuclear fuels train past Wandel, north of Abington on the WCML, on 21 May 2019. *Robin Ralston*

88005	aeup*	XHVE	BEA	DRE	CR	*Minerva*
88006	aeup*	XHVE	BEA	DRE	CR	*Juno*
88007	aeup*	XHVE	BEA	DRE	CR	*Electra*
88008	aeup*	XHVE	BEA	DRE	CR	*Ariadne*
88009	aeup*	XHVE	BEA	DRE	CR	*Diana*
88010	aeup*	XHVE	BEA	DRE	CR	*Aurora*

Class 90

An enhanced version of the Class 87 – the 90s were originally going to be Class 87/2s. Fifteen locos remain in passenger use with Greater Anglia but will be replaced in 2020 and 13 are due to transfer to Freightliner to join the ten locos already in its fleet and two – 90001/002 are expected to transfer to LSL. The remainder are in freight use with DB Cargo, but withdrawals started over a decade ago.

Built by:	BREL Crewe
Years introduced:	1987-90
Wheel arrangement:	Bo-Bo
Weight:	84.5 tons
Length:	61ft 6in (18.74m)
Power supply:	25kV AC
Control system:	Thyristor
Traction output (max):	7,680hp (5,860kW)
Traction output (con):	5,000hp (3,730kW)
Tractive effort:	58,000lb
ETH index:	95
Maximum design speed:	110mph (176km/h)

When the WCML is closed at nights, Caledonian Sleeper trains use King's Cross instead of Euston. That was the case on 19 August as Freightliner's 90048 waits to leave with 1S66, the 2118 to Inverness. These trains are now exclusively worked by Class 92s south of Edinburgh. *Graeme Elgar*

Brake Force:	40 tons					
Route Availability:	7					
Traction Motor type:	GEC G412CY					
Multiple Working type:	TDM					

90001	aeu	IANA	POR	AGA	NC	*Crown Point*
90002	aeu	IANA	POR	AGA	NC	*Eastern Daily Press 1870-2010 SERVING NORFOLK FOR 140 YEARS*
90003	aeu	IANA	POR	AGA	NC	
90004	aeu	IANA	POR	AGA	NC	*City of Chelmsford*
90005	aeu	IANA	POR	AGA	NC	*Vice-Admiral Lord Nelson*
90006	aeu	IANA	POR	AGA	NC	*Roger Ford/Modern Railways Magazine*
90007	aeu	IANA	POR	AGA	NC	*Sir John Betjeman*
90008	aeu	IANA	POR	AGA	NC	*The East Anglian*
90009	aeu	IANA	POR	AGA	NC	
90010	aeu	IANA	POR	AGA	NC	
90011	aeu	IANA	POR	AGA	NC	*East Anglian Daily Times – Suffolk & Proud*
90012	aeu	IANA	POR	AGA	NC	*Royal Anglian Regiment*
90013	aeu	IANA	POR	AGA	NC	
90014	aeu	IANA	POR	AGA	NC	*Norfolk & Norwich Festival*
90015	aeu	IANA	POR	AGA	NC	*Colchester Castle*
90016	aeu	DFLC	POR	FLR	CB	
90017	aeu	WQBA	DBC	EWS	CE (U)	
90018	aeu	WQAA	DBC	DBS	CE (S)	*The Pride of Bellshill*
90019	aeu	WEDC	DBC	DBC	CE	*Multimodal*

90020		aeu	WEDC	DBC	EWS	CE	Collingwood
90021	90221	aeu	WQAB	DBC	FSR	CE (U)	
90022	90222	aeu	WQBA	DBC	REW	CE (U)	Freightconnection
90023	90223	aeu	WQBA	DBC	RFE	CE (U)	
90024	90224	aeu	WQAB	DBC	MAA	CE (U)	
90025	90125, 90225	aeu	WQBA	DBC	RFD	CE (U)	
90026	90126	aeu	WQBA	DBC	EWS	CE (U)	
90027	90127, 90227	aeu	WQBA	DBC	RFD	CE (U)	Allerton T&RS Depot
90028	90128	aeu	WEDC	DBC	DBC	CE	Sir William McAlpine
90029	90129	aeu	WEDC	DBC	DBC	CE	
90030	90130	aeu	WQBA	DBC	EWS	CE (U)	
90031	90131	aeu	WQBA	DBC	EWS	CE (U)	The Railway Children Partnership: Working for Street Children Worldwide
90032	90132	aeu	WQBA	DBC	EWS	CE (U)	
90033	90133, 90233	aeu	WQBA	DBC	RFE	CE (U)	
90034	90134	aeu	WEDC	DBC	DRU	CE	
90035	90135	aeu	WQAA	DBC	DBC	TO (S)	
90036	90136	aeu	WQAA	DBC	DBC	CE (S)	Driver Jack Mills
90037	90137	aeu	WEAC	DBC	EWS	CE	Spirit of Dagenham
90038	90138, 90238	aeu	WQBA	DBC	RFE	CE (U)	
90039	90139, 90239	aeu	WEDC	DBC	EWS	CE	
90040	90140	aeu	WEDC	DBC	DBC	CE	
90041	90141	aeu	DFLC	POR	FLR	CB	
90042	90142	aeu	DFLC	POR	FPH	CB	
90043	90143	aeu	DFLC	POR	FPH	CB	
90044	90144	aeu	DFLC	POR	FLG	CB	
90045	90145	aeu	DFLC	POR	FPH	CB	
90046	90146	aeu	DFLC	POR	FLR	CB	
90047	90147	aeu	DFLC	POR	FLG	CB	
90048	90148	aeu	DFLC	POR	FLG	CB	
90049	90149	aeu	DFLC	POR	FPH	CB	
90050	90150	aeu	DHLT	ARV	TTG	CB (U)	

Class 91

Dedicated express passenger locos for the East Coast Main Line, they are now being replaced by new IEP EMUs and withdrawals have started, although locos may remain in 'active' pools even when stood down. Redeployment or disposal will then be inevitable and many are expected to be exported to Eastern Europe. All were built as 91/0s but refurbished in 2001-03 and renumbered in the 91/1 series.

Built by:	BREL Crewe
Years introduced:	1988-91
Wheel arrangement:	Bo-Bo
Weight:	84 tons
Length:	63ft 8in (19.40m)
Power supply:	25kV AC
Control system:	Thyristor
Traction output (max):	6,300hp (4,700kW)
Traction output (con):	6,090hp (4,540kW)
ETH index:	95
Maximum operating speed:	125mph (200km/h) restricted to 110mph (176km/h) when flat end leading
Brake Force:	45 tons
Route Availability:	7

Time is running out for Class 91s on ECML passenger workings and the first have now been returned to their rolling stock leasing company. On 15 April 2016, 91111 *For the Fallen* passes Claypole as it heads to Edinburgh. *Bill Atkinson*

Traction Motor type: GEC G426AZ
Multiple Working type: TDM

91101	91001	aeu	IECA	EVS	VFS	BN	*FLYING SCOTSMAN*
91102	91002	aeu	IECA	EVS	VEC	BN	*City of York*
91103	91003	aeu	IECA	EVS	VEA	BN (S)	
91104	91004	aeu	IECA	EVS	VEC	BN	
91105	91005	aeu	IECA	EVS	VEC	BN	
91106	91006	aeu	IECA	EVS	VEA	BN	
91107	91007	aeu	IECA	EVS	VEC	BN	*SKYFALL*
91108	91008	aeu	IECA	EVS	VEC	ZF (U)	
91109	91009	aeu	IECA	EVS	VEC	BN	*Sir Bobby Robson*
91110	91010	aeu	IECA	EVS	BBM	BN	*BATTLE OF BRITAIN MEMORIAL FLIGHT*
91111	91011	aeu	IECA	EVS	FTF	BN	*For the Fallen*
91112	91012	aeu	IECA	EVS	VEC	BN	
91113	91013	aeu	IECA	EVS	VEC	BN	
91114	91014	aeu	IECA	EVS	VEA	BN	*Durham Cathedral*
91115	91015	aeu	IECA	EVS	VEC	BN	*Blaydon Races*
91116	91016	aeu	IECA	EVS	VEC	BN	
91117	91017	aeu	IECA	EVS	EPX	LR (S)	
91118	91018	aeu	IECA	EVS	VEC	BN	*The Fusiliers*
91119	91019	aeu	IECA	EVS	ICS	BN	*Bounds Green INTERCITY Depot 1977-2017*
91120	91020	aeu	IECA	EVS	EPX	LR (S)	
91121	91021	aeu	IECA	EVS	VEC	BN	
91122	91022	aeu	IECA	EVS	VEC	BN	
91124	91024	aeu	IECA	EVS	VEC	BN	
91125	91025	aeu	IECA	EVS	VEC	BN	
91126	91026	aeu	IECA	EVS	VEC	BN	*Darlington Hippodrome*
91127	91027	aeu	IECA	EVS	VEC	BN	

91128	91028	aeu	IECA	EVS	VEC	BN	
91129	91029	aeu	IECA	EVS	VEC	BN	
91130	91030	aeu	IECA	EVS	VEC	BN	*Lord Mayor of Newcastle*
91131	91031	aeu	IECA	EVS	VEC	BN	
91132	91023	aeu	IECA	EVS	VEA	BN	

91103 has Celebrating Pride graphics
91106 has Great Exhibition of the North graphics
91114 has Durham Cathedral graphics
91121 has Trainbow branding
91132 has 'time to change Employer Pledge' branding

Class 92

A fleet of 46 locos were ordered for Channel Tunnel work, but much of the traffic never materialised and the locos were woefully underutilised and many withdrawn from 2001. Seven were owned by Eurostar, nine by SNCF and 30 by BR's Railfreight Distribution sector. The latter all transferred to EWS while GBRf has bought the other 16. Several ex-DB Cargo locos are now in Bulgaria and Romania. Two withdrawn locos have recently been returned to traffic by GBRf after overhauls, but disposal of the remaining four is possible.

Built by:	Brush Traction
Years introduced:	1993-95
Wheel arrangement:	Co-Co
Weight:	126 tons
Length:	70ft 1in (21.34m)
Power supply:	25kV AC or 750V DC
Control system:	Asynchronous 3-phase
Traction output (max):	6,700hp (5,000kW) – overhead power supply
	5,360hp (4,000kW) - third rail power supply
Tractive effort:	Normal – 81,000lbf; boost – 90,000lbf
ETH index:	108
Maximum design speed:	87mph (139km/h)
Brake Force:	63 tons
Route Availability:	8
Traction Motor type:	Brush
Multiple working type:	not fitted

92004	ae	WQBA	DBC	EUE	CE (U)	*Jane Austen*
92006	aed	GBSL	GBR	CAL	WN	
92007	ae	WQBA	DBC	EUK	CE (U)	*Schubert*
92008	ae	WQBA	DBC	EUE	CE (U)	*Jules Verne*
92009	ae	WQBA	DBC	DBC	CE (U)	*Elgar*
92010	aed	GBST	GBR	CAL	WN	
92011	ae	WFBC	DBC	EUE	CE	*Handel*
92013	ae	WQAB	DBC	EUE	CE (U)	*Puccini*
92014	aed	GBSL	GBR	CAL	WN	
92015	ae	WFBC	DBC	DBC	CE	
92016	ae	WQAA	DBC	DBC	CE (U)	
92017	ae	WQBA	DBC	STO	CE (U)	*Bart the Engine*
92018	aed	GBST	GBR	CAL	WN	
92019	ae	WFBC	DBC	EUE	CE	*Wagner*
92020	aed	GBSL	GBR	GBR	WN	
92021	ae	GBSD	GBR	EUK	BL (U)	*Purcell*
92023	ae	GBSL	GBR	CAL	WN	
92028	aed	GBST	GBR	GBR	WN	

92029	ae	WQAB	DBC	EUE	CE (U)	Dante
92031	ae	WQBA	DBC	DBC	CE (U)	The Institute of Logistics & Transport
92032	ae	GBST	GBR	GBR	WN	IMechE Railway Division
92033	aed	GBSL	GBR	CAL	WN	
92035	ae	WQBA	DBC	EUK	CE (U)	Mendelssohn
92036	ae	WFBC	DBC	EUE	CE	Bertolt Brecht
92037	ae	WQBA	DBC	EUE	CE (U)	Sullivan
92038	aed	GBST	GBR	CAL	WN	
92040	ae	GBSD	GBR	EUK	BL (U)	Goethe
92041	ae	WFBC	DBC	EUE	CE	Vaughan Williams
92042	ae	WFBC	DBC	DBC	CE	
92043	aed	GBST	GBR	GBR	WN	
92044	ae	GBST	GBR	EUK	WN	Couperin
92045	ae	GBSD	GBR	EUK	BL (U)	Chaucer
92046	ae	GBSD	GBR	EUK	BL (U)	Sweelinck

Note: Nos 92009-011/015/016/018/019/023/031/032/036/038/041-043 have TVM430 in-cab signalling equipment fitted for working on HS1 lines.

In Caledonian Sleeper livery, but owned and operated by GB Railfreight, 92014 passes Hornsey with 5E43, the 0855 King's Cross-Wembley ECS on 4 May 2019. *Graeme Elgar*

2 Spot hire and industrial locos

This section lists all locos regarded as available for short-term or medium-term spot hire but do not have full main line registration, plus locos that have been sold or moved abroad on a long term basis. Not all locos are necessarily operation and some may be disposed of.

Loco's current TOPS number	Previous official numbers carried	Key detail differences	Current TOPS Sector	Vehicle Owner	Current Livery	Current depot allocation or location	Current name (as displayed on the loco) Minor wording on crests, plaques or graphics is excluded
Class 03
03084	D2084	xow		CRB	GWS	CS	
03196	D2196	xow		WCR	GNY	CS	
	D2381	vo		WCR	GNY	CS (U)	
Class 07
07007	D2991	vo	MBDL	AFS	BRW	ZG	
07011	D2995	xow		SLE	GWS	SE	
Class 08
08021	D3029, 13029	vo		TLW	BLK	TM	
08168	D3236, 13236	vo		NEM	BLK	EOR	
08220	D3290, 13290	vo		EEG	BRW	ZW	
08296	D3955, 08787	xo		AGI	BLE	MQ (U)	
08308	D3378	ao	MRSO	RMS	FSR	PD	
08375	D3460	ao	MBDL	RMS	BLK	SS	
08389	D3504	ao	HNRS	HNR	EWS	CC	
08401	D3516	ao		HUN	HUN	HH	
08405	D3520	ao	MBDL	DBC	EWR	NL	
08423	D3538	ao		RMS	RMS	PD	
08428	D3543	ao	HNRL	HNR	EWS	BH (U)	
08441	D3556	ao	MBDL	RSS	RSS	BN	
08442	D3557	ao		ARV	LNW	EH (U)	
08445	D3560	ao		HUN	MAL	DD	
08447	D3562	ao		DST	DST	DS	
08460	D3575	ao	MBDL	RSS	RSS	LP	*SPIRIT OF THE OAK*
08484	D3599	ao	MBDL	RSS	RSS	WC	*CAPTAIN NATHANIEL DARELL*
08499	D3654	ao		PUL	BLE	CF	*REDLIGHT*
08500	D3655	ao	HNRL	HNR	EWS	BU (U)	
08502	D3657	ao	HNRL	HNR	NOR	BH	
08503	D3658	ao	HNRL	HNC	BLU	BIR	
08516	D3678	ao		ARV	LNW	BK	*RORY*
08527	D3689	ao	HNRL	HNR	TTG	AR	
08536	D3700	xo	HISE	RSS	BRW	WI (U)	
08567	D3734	ao	MBDL	AFS	EWS	ZG	
08568	D3735	xo	MBDL	KBR	RCG	ZH	*St Rollox*
08573	D3740	xo	MRSO	RMS	BLK	WO	
08578	D3745	ao	HNRS	HNR	EWS	LM (U)	
08580	D3747	xo	MBDL	RSS	EWS	BN	
08593	D3760	ao	MBDL	RSS	EWS	WI (U)	
08598	D3765	ao		POT		WI (U)	
08600	D3767, 97800	ao		AVD	AVD	MB	
08602	D3769	ao		BOM	BLE	ZD	

71

08613	D3780	ao		RMS	RMS	WO	
08615	D3782	ao	RFSH	HUN	HUN	SS	*Uncle Dai*
08622	D3789	ao		RMS	BLK	KT	
08623	D3790	ao		HNR	DBS	HO (U)	
08629	D3796	xo	RCZN	KBR	KBR	ZN	*Wolverton*
08630	D3797	ao	HNRL	HNR	CEL	CC	*Celsa Endeavour*
08632	D3799	ao	MBDL	RSS	RSS	TR	
08643	D3810	xo	MBDL	AGI	GRE	MD	
08649	D3816	xo	RCZN	KBR	KBR	ZN	*Bradwell*
08650	D3817	xo		AGI	BRY	WI	
08652	D3819	ao		AGI	BRY	MD	
08653	D3820	xo	HNRS	HNR	EWS	LM (U)	
08663	D3830	ao		BRW		WI (U)	
08669	D3836	ao	RFSH	WAB	BLK	ZB	*Bob Machin*
08676	D3843	xo	HNRL	HNR	EWS	EKR	
08682	D3849	xo	KDSD	BOM	SPE	ZD	*Lionheart*
08685	D3852	ao	HNRS	HNR	EWS	EKR	
08700	D3867	xo		HNR	BRW	ZI	
08701	D3868	xo	HNRS	HNR	RES	LM (U)	
08703	D3870	ao	MBDL	RSS	EWS	SP	
08706	D3873	ao		HNR	EWS	WI (U)	
08709	D3876	xo	MBDL	RSS	EWS	WI (U)	
08711	D3878	ao	HNRS	HNR	RES	BU (U)	
08714	D3881	ao	MBDL	HNR	EWS	HO (U)	
08724	D3892	xo	HBSH	WAB	BLK	ZB	
08730	D3898	xo	RCZH	KBR	KBR	ZN	
08742	D3910	ao	HNRL	HNR	RES	DRC	
08743	D3911	ao	MBDL	ICI	BLE	BB	*Bryan Turner*
08752	D3920	ao	MBDL	RSS	EWS	ZN	
08756	D3924	ao	MRSO	RMS	DEP	SS	
08757	D3925	ao	WQBA	RSS	RES	DG	
08762	D3930	ao	MRSO	RMS	BLK	DF	
08765	D3933	ao	HNRS	HNR	HNO	BH (U)	
08774	D3942	ao		AVD	AVD	MB	*ARTHUR VERNON DAWSON*
08782	D3950	ao	HNRL	HNR	COR	BH (U)	
08783	D3951	ao		EMR	EWS	ZO (U)	
08784	D3952	ao	MBDL		EWS	WI (U)	
08786	D3954	ao	HNRS	HNR	DEP	BH (U)	
08788	D3956	ao	MRSO	RMS	RMS	WO	
08798	D3966	ao		EMR	EWS	AT (U)	
08799	D3967	ao		HNR	EWS	EK	
08802	D3971	ao	HNRS	HNR	EWS	WI (U)	
08804	D3972	ao	WQDA	HNR	EWS	EK	
08809	D3977	xo	MRSO	RMS	RMS	PD	
08823	D3991	ao	KDSD	HUN	HEO	SS	*KELVA*
08824	D3992	ao	HNRL	HNR	BLK	BH (U)	
08846	D4014	xo		BOM	BLE	NL	
08847	D4015	xow	MBDL	RMS	COT	NC	
08853	D4021	ao	RFSH	WAB	BLK	ZB	
08865	D4033	ao	HNRL	HNR	EWS	HO (U)	
08870	D4038	xo	MBDL	RMS	CAS	KT	
08871	D4039	xo	MBDL	RMS	COT	ZI	
08872	D4040	xo		EMR	EWS	AT	
08873	D4041	ao	DDIN	HUN	RES	LH (U)	
08874	D4042	xo	MBDL	RMS	SIL	SS	
08877	D4045	xo	HNRS	HNR	DEP	BH	*WIGAN 1*
08879	D4047	xo	WQAA	AFS	EWS	ZG	

08885	D4115	xo		RMS	RMS	WO (U)	
08892	D4122	xod	HNRL	HNR	DRS	AH	
08903	D4133	ao	MBDL	ICI	BLE	BB	*John W Antill*
08904	D4134	ao	HNRL	HNR	EWS	CC	
08905	D4135	ao	HNRS	HNR	EWS	HO (U)	
08912	D4142	ao		AVD	BRW	MB (U)	
08913	D4143	ao		RMS	MAL	ZO (U)	
08918	D4148	xo	HNRS	HNR	DEP	BU (U)	
08921	D4151	ao		RSS	EWS	WI (U)	
08924	D4154	ao	HNRS	HNR	GBR	BH	
08927	D4157	xo	MBDL	AGO	GWS	WI	
08933	D4163	aow		AGI	BRY	MD	
08936	D4166	ao	MBDL	RMS	RMS	SS	
08939	D4169	ao	MBDL	RSS	RSS	FX	
08943	D4173	xo	HNRL	HNR	HNR	CZ	
08944	D4174	xo		HNR	BLK	BQ (U)	
08947	D4177	ao		AGI	BRY	MD	
08956	D4186	xo	CDJD	SEC	BRW	WI	
08994	D3577, 08462	ao	HNRS	HNR	EWS	BU (U)	
08995	D3854, 08687	ao			EWS	WI (U)	

08738 is fitted with nose end scaffolding and AAR multiple working
08428/511/578/588/630/652/685/703/706/711/737/762/824/905/924/947 have swinghead couplers

Class 09

09006	D3670	xo	HNRS	HNR	EWS	BU (U)	
09014	D4102	xo	HNRS	HNR	DEP	BU (U)	
09022	D4110	ao		VIC	BDB	BD	
09023	D4111	ao		EMR	EWS	AT (U)	
09106	D3927, 08759	ao	HNRL	HNR	HNR	DG	
09201	D3536, 08421	ao	HNRL	HNR	DEP	HO (U)	
09204	D3884, 08717	ao	MBDL	ARV	ARV	CP	

09023/106/201 have swinghead couplers

Class 20

20016	D8016	xo	HNRS	HNR	BRB	LM (U)	
20056	D8056	ao	HNRL	HNR	COY	SC (U)	
20066	D8066	ao		HNR	TAT	HO (U)	
20069	D8069	xo		IINR	BRB	MNR (U)	
20081	D8081	xop	HNRS	HNR	BRB	LM (U)	
20087	D8087	xop	MBDL	HNR	BRB	BQ (U)	
20088	D8088	xop	HNRS	HNR	RFS	LM (U)	
20110	D8110	xop		HNR	GYP	BQ (U)	
20121	D8121	aop	HNRS	HNR	HNO	BH (U)	
20166	D8166	aop	HNRL	HNR	HNO	WR	
20168	D8168, 20304	aop	HNRL	HNR	HOP	HO	*SIR GEORGE EARLE*
20903	D8083, 20083	aotp	HNRS	HNR	DRU	BU (U)	
20904	D8041, 20041	aotp	HNRS	HNR	DRU	BU (U)	
20906	D8319, 20219	aotp	HNRL	HNR	HOP	HO	

Note: 20121 has been modified with a shunter's verandha at No. 2 end. The loco is not operational

Class 25

25057	D5207	xbp		HNR	BRB	NNR (U)	
25278	D7628	xo	MBDL	NYM	GYP	GO	*SYBILLA*
25283	D7633, 25904	xop	MBDL	HNR	GYP	RFL (U)	
25313	D7663	xop		HNR	BRB	WR (U)	

Class 31

31454	D5684, 31256	xe		HNR	ICM	WO (U)	
31459	D5684, 31256	xe	RVLO	HNR	BRB	WO	
31461	D5547, 31129	xe	NRLO	NEM	CCE	BU (U)	

Class 37

37146	D6846	xop	MBDL	EPX	CCE	LR (U)	
37198	D6898	xotp	MBDL	NET	NRY	DF (U)	
37207	D6907	xotp	MBDL	EPX	BRB	LR (U)	
37240	D6940	xotp		BOD	UND	NM (U)	
37255	D6955	xotp	NRLS	NEM	CCE	BU (U)	

Class 47

47488	D1713	xet	NRLS	NEM	GYP	BU	
47701	D1932, 47493	xet	NRLO	NEM	TWO	BU (U)	*Waverley*
47703	D1960, 47514	xet	HNRS	HNR	UND	ZF (U)	
47714	D1955, 47511	xet	HNRL	HNR	ANG	AH	
47715	D1945, 47502	xet	MBDL	HNR	NSD	WK	*Haymarket*
47744	D1927, 47250, 47600	xet	NRLS	NEM	EWS	BU (U)	
47769	D1753, 47491	xetm	HNRS	HNR	VIR	BH (U)	*Resolve*

Class 66

66048		aost		EMD	UND	ZW (U)	

Class 73

73133	E6040	xew	MBED	TMT	TMT	BM	

Class 86

86229	E3119	ae	EPEX	FLI	VIR	CB (U)	
86251	E3101	ae	EPEX	FLI	VIR	CB (U)	

Europhoenix has several Class 37s that are hired to ROG. No. 37601 *Perseus* passes Kempston Hardwick on 30 January 2019. This is an ex-Eurostar and then DRS loco and is the oldest Class 37 still in day-to-day use. *Paul Shannon*

No. 47773 is owned by Vintage Trains and used for working its own excursions now the company has become a fully-fledged Train Operating Company. The loco was at Tyseley on 18 September 2018. *Pip Dunn*

No. 73133 is owned by Transmart Trains and has been used for shunting at Bournemouth Depot. On 4 January 2019 it was at the Arlington works at Eastleigh. *Mark Pike*

Exported locomotives

Loco's current number	Previous UK numbers	Key detail difference	Current TOPS Sector	Vehicle Owner	Current Livery	Current depot allocation or location	Current name
Class 03							
D2156	03156	vo		ITY	BLU		
Class 08							
D3047	13047	vo		LAM	LAM		
D3092	13092	vo		LAM	LAM		
Note: Both these locos may have been scrapped							
Class 47							
92 70 00 47375-5	47375, D1894	aot	NRLO	CON	CSM	HUN	*FALCON*
Class 56							
92 55 0659 001-5	56101	ao		FLY	FLY	HUN	
92 55 0659 002-3	56115	ao		FLY	FLY	HUN	
92 55 0659 003-1	56117	ao		FLY	FER	HUN (U)	

Class 58

	58001	aosp	WQCA	DBC	ETF	AZ (U)	
	58004	aosp	WQCA	DBC	TSO	AZ (U)	
	58005	aosp	WQCA	DBC	ETF	AZ (U)	
	58006	aosp	WQCA	DBC	ETF	AZ (U)	
	58007	aosp	WQCA	DBC	TSO	AZ (U)	
	58009	aosp	WQCA	DBC	TSO	AZ (U)	
	58010	aosp	WQCA	DBC	TSO	AZ (U)	
	58011	aosp	WQCA	DBC	TSO	AZ (U)	
	58013	aosp	WQCA	DBC	ETF	AZ (U)	
L54	58015	aosp		TFA	CON	AC	
	58018	aosp	WQCA	DBC	TSO	AZ (U)	
L43	58020	aosp		TFA	CON	AC	
	58021	aosp	WQCA	DBC	ETF	AZ (U)	
L42	58024	aosp		TFA	CON	AC	
	58025	aosp	WQCA	DBC	CON	AB (U)	
	58026	aosp	WQCA	DBC	TSO	AZ (U)	
L52	58027	aosp	WQCA	DBC	CON	AB (U)	
L44	58029	aosp		TFA	CON	AC (U)	
L46	58030	aosp		TFA	CON	AC	
L45	58031	aosp		TFA	CON	AC	Caballero Ferroviario
	58032	aosp	WQCA	DBC	ETF	AZ (U)	
	58033	aosp	WQCA	DBC	TSO	AZ (U)	
	58034	aosp	WQCA	DBC	TSO	AZ (U)	
	58035	aosp	WQCA	DBC	TSO	AZ (U)	
	58036	aosp	WQCA	DBC	ETF	AZ (U)	
5814	58038	aosp	WQCA	TFA	ETF	AZ (U)	
5811	58039	aosp	WQCA	DBC	ETF	AZ (U)	
	58040	aosp	WQCA	DBC	TSO	AZ (U)	
L36	58041	aosp		TFA	CON	AB (U)	
	58042	aosp	WQCA	DBC	ETF	AZ (U)	
L37	58043	aosp		TFA	CON	AC	
5812	58044	aosp	WQCA	DBC	ETF	WP (U)	
	58046	aosp	WQCA	DBC	TSO	AZ (U)	
L51	58047	aosp		TFA	CON	AC	
	58049	aosp	WQCA	DBC	ETF	AZ (U)	
L53	58050	aosp	WQCA	DBC	CON	AB (U)	

There are 23 DB Cargo Class 58s all dumped at Alizay in France after their hire contracts for infrastructure work ended. No. 58033 heads lines of locos on 14 April 2016. *Paul Fuller*

Class 66

92 70 0 066010-4	66010	aos	WGEA	DBC	EWS	AZ
92 70 0 066022-9	66022	aos	WGEA	DBC	EWS	AZ
92 70 0 066026-0	66026	aos	WGEA	DBC	EWS	AZ
92 70 0 066028-6	66028	aos	WGEA	DBC	EWS	AZ
92 70 0 066029-4	66029	aos	WGEA	DBC	EWS	AZ
92 70 0 066032-8	66032	aos	WGEA	DBC	EWS	AZ
92 70 0 066033-6	66033	aos	WGEA	DBC	EWS	AZ
92 70 0 066036-9	66036	aos	WGEA	DBC	EWS	AZ
92 70 0 066038-5	66038	aos	WGEA	DBC	EWS	AZ
92 70 0 066042-7	66042	aos	WGEA	DBC	EWS	AZ
92 70 0 066045-0	66045	aos	WGEA	DBC	EWS	AZ
92 70 0 066049-2	66049	aos	WGEA	DBC	EWS	AZ
92 70 0 066052-6	66052	aos	WGEA	DBC	EWS	AZ
92 70 0 066062-5	66062	aos	WGEA	DBC	EWS	AZ
92 70 0 066064-1	66064	aos	WGEA	DBC	EWS	AZ
92 70 0 066071-6	66071	aos	WGEA	DBC	EWS	AZ
92 70 0 066072-4	66072	aos	WGEA	DBC	EWS	AZ
92 70 0 066073-2	66073	aos	WGEA	DBC	EWS	AZ
92 70 0 066123-5	66123	aos	WGEA	DBC	EWS	AZ
92 70 0 066146-6	66146	aos	WGEP	DBC	EWS	PN
92 70 0 066153-2	66153	aos	WGEP	DBC	EWS	PN
92 70 0 066157-3	66157	aos	WGEP	DBC	EWS	PN
92 70 0 066159-9	66159	aos	WGEP	DBC	EWS	PN
92 70 0 066163-1	66163	aos	WGEP	DBC	DBR	PN
92 70 0 066166-4	66166	aos	WGEP	DBC	EWS	PN
92 70 0 066173-0	66173	aos	WGEP	DBC	EWS	PN
92 70 0 066178-9	66178	aos	WGEP	DBC	DBR	PN
92 70 0 066179-7	66179	aos	WGEA	DBC	EWS	AZ
92 70 0 066180-5	66180	aos	WGEP	DBC	EWS	PN
92 70 0 066189-6	66189	aos	WGEP	DBC	DBR	PN
92 70 0 066190-4	66190	aos	WGEA	DBC	EWS	AZ
92 70 0 066191-2	66191	aos	WGEA	DBC	EWS	AZ
92 70 0 066193-8	66193	aos	WGEA	DBC	EWS	AZ
92 70 0 066195-3	66195	aos	WGEA	DBC	EWS	AZ
92 70 0 066196-1	66196	aos	WGEP	DBC	EWS	PN
92 70 0 066201-9	66201	aos	WGEA	DBC	EWS	AZ
92 70 0 066202-7	66202	aos	WGEA	DBC	EWS	AZ
92 70 0 066203-5	66203	aos	WGEA	DBC	EWS	AZ
92 70 0 066204-3	66204	aos	WGEA	DBC	EWS	AZ
92 70 0 066205-1	66205	aos	WGEA	DBC	EWS	AZ
92 70 0 066208-4	66208	aos	WGEA	DBC	EWS	AZ
92 70 0 066209-2	66209	aos	WGEA	DBC	EWS	AZ
92 70 0 066210-0	66210	aos	WGEA	DBC	EWS	AZ
92 70 0 066211-8	66211	aos	WGEA	DBC	EWS	AZ
92 70 0 066212-6	66212	aos	WGEA	DBC	EWS	AZ
92 70 0 066213-4	66213	aos	WGEA	DBC	EWS	AZ
92 70 0 066214-2	66214	aos	WGEA	DBC	EWS	AZ
92 70 0 066215-9	66215	aos	WGEA	DBC	EWS	AZ
92 70 0 066216-7	66216	aos	WGEA	DBC	EWS	AZ
92 70 0 066217-5	66217	aos	WGEA	DBC	EWS	AZ
92 70 0 066218-3	66218	aos	WGEA	DBC	EWS	AZ
92 70 0 066219-1	66219	aos	WGEA	DBC	EWS	AZ
92 70 0 066220-9	66220	aos	WGEP	DBC	DBR	PN
92 70 0 066222-5	66222	aos	WGEA	DBC	EWS	AZ

92 70 0 066223-3	66223	aos	WGEA	DBC	EWS	AZ	
92 70 0 066224-1	66224	aos	WGEA	DBC	EWS	AZ	
92 70 0 066225-8	66225	aos	WGEA	DBC	EWS	AZ	
92 70 0 066226-6	66226	aos	WGEA	DBC	EWS	AZ	
92 70 0 066227-4	66227	aos	WGEP	DBC	DBR	PN	
92 70 0 066228-2	66228	aos	WGEA	DBC	EWS	AZ	
92 70 0 066229-0	66229	aos	WGEA	DBC	EWS	AZ	
92 70 0 066231-6	66231	aos	WGEA	DBC	EWS	AZ	
92 70 0 066232-4	66232	aos	WGEA	DBC	EWS	AZ	
92 70 0 066233-2	66233	aos	WGEA	DBC	EWS	AZ	
92 70 0 066234-0	66234	aos	WGEA	DBC	EWS	AZ	
92 70 0 066235-7	66235	aos	WGEA	DBC	EWS	AZ	
92 70 0 066236-5	66236	aos	WGEA	DBC	EWS	AZ	
92 70 0 066237-3	66237	aos	WGEP	DBC	EWS	PN	
92 70 0 066239-9	66239	aos	WGEA	DBC	EWS	AZ	
92 70 0 066240-7	66240	aos	WGEA	DBC	EWS	AZ	
92 70 0 066241-5	66241	aos	WGEA	DBC	EWS	AZ	
92 70 0 066242-3	66242	aos	WGEA	DBC	EWS	AZ	
92 70 0 066243-1	66243	aos	WGEA	DBC	EWS	AZ	
92 70 0 066244-9	66244	aos	WGEA	DBC	EWS	AZ	
92 70 0 066245-6	66245	aos	WGEA	DBC	EWS	AZ	
92 70 0 066246-4	66246	aos	WGEA	DBC	EWS	AZ	
92 70 0 066247-2	66247	aos	WGEA	DBC	EWS	AZ	
92 70 0 066248-9	66248	aos	WGEP	DBC	DBR	PN	
92 70 0 066249-8	66249	aos	WGEA	DBC	EWS	AZ	
66013	66411	aos	DHLT	MAQ	FPH	FP	
66015	66412	aos	DHLT	MAQ	FPH	FP	
66014	66417	aos	DHLT	MAQ	FPH	FP	
66016	66527	aos	DHLT	EVS	FLR	FP	
66017	66530	aos	DHLT	POR	FLR	FP	
66018	66535	aos	DHLT	POR	FLR	FP	
66009	66582	aos	DHLT	EVS	FLR	FP	
66010	66583	aos	DHLT	EVS	FLR	FP	
66011	66584	aos	DHLT	EVS	FLR	FP	
66008	66586	aos	DHLT	MAQ	FLR	FP	
	66595	aos	DHLT	BEA	FLR	FP	
66603	66608	aos	DHLT	POR	FLR	FP	
66605	66609	aos	DHLT	POR	FLR	FP	
66604	66611	aos	DHLT	POR	FLR	FP	
66606	66612	aos	DHLT	POR	FLR	FP	
66602	66624	aos	DHLT	MAQ	FLR	FP	
66601	66625	aos	DHLT	MAQ	FLR	FP	
	66954	aos	DHLT	BEA	FLR	FP	

Note: The Freightliner Poland locos have been renumbered in the 660xx series for Class 66/5s and 6660x series for Class 66/6s. FPL also owns seven 'Class 66s' numbered 66001-007, which were new-build locos and did not work in the UK

DB Cargo's Euro Cargo Rail subsidiary also operates 60 'Class 66s', numbered 77001-060, which were new-build locos and did not work in the UK

All WGEP locos have their swinghead couplers removed. WGEA locos retain them

Class 86

91 52 00 85003-2	86213, E3193	ae	BMT	BMT	BUL	*Lancashire Witch*
91 55 0450 005-6	86215, E3165	ae	FLY	FLY	HUN	
91 55 0450 006-6	86217, 86504, E3177	ae	FLY	FLY	HUN	

91 55 0450 004-1	86218, E3175	ae	FLY	FLY	HUN		
91 55 0450 007-4	86228, E3167	ae	FLY	FLY	HUN		
9152 00 85005-2	86231, E3126	ae	BMT	BMT	BUL	*Lady of the Lake*	
91 55 0450 003-3	86232, E3113	ae	FLY	FLY	HUN		
	86233, 86506, E3172	ae	BMT	EBY	BUL (U)		
9152 00 85006-2	86234, E3155	ae	BMT	BMT	BUL		
9152 00 85004-7	86235, E3194	ae	BMT	BMT	BUL	*Novelty*	
91 55 0450 008-2	86242, E3138	ae	FLY	FLY	HUN		
91 55 0450 001-7	86248, E3107	ae	FLY	FLY	HUN		
91 55 0450 002-5	86250, E3189	ae	FLY	FLY	HUN		
91 55 0450 009-0	86424, E3111, 86024, 86324	ae	FLY	NRY	HUN (U)		
91 52 00 85001-6	86701, E3128, 86205, 86503	ae	BMT	BMT	BUL	*Orion*	
91 52 00 85002-4	86702 E3144, 86048, 86260	ae	BMT	BMT	BUL	*Cassiopeia*	

Class 87

91 52 00 87003-7	87003	ae	BZK	BZK	BUL		
91 52 00 87004-5	87004	ae	BZK	BRZ	BUL	*Britannia*	
91 52 00 87006-0	87006	ae	BZK	DGB	BUL (U)		
91 52 00 87007-8	87007	ae	BZK	COT	BUL		
91 52 00 87008-9	87008	ae	BZK	COT	BUL (U)		
91 52 00 87009-4	87009	ae	BMT	BMT	BUL		
91 52 00 87010-2	87010	ae	BZK	BZK	BUL		
91 52 00 87012-8	87012	ae	BZK	NSE	BUL		
91 52 00 87013-6	87013	ae	BZK	BZK	BUL		
91 52 00 87014-7	87014	ae	BZK	BZK	BUL (U)		
91 52 00 87017-7	87017	ae	BMT	EPX	BUL	*Iron Duke*	
91 52 00 87019-3	87019	ae	BZK	LNR	RUL		
91 52 00 87020-1	87020	ae	BZK	BZK	BUL		
91 52 00 87022-7	87022	ae	BZK	DGB	BUL		
91 52 00 87023-5	87023	ae	BMT	EPX	BUL	*Velocity*	
91 52 00 87025-0	87025	ae	BMT	BMT	BUL		
91 52 00 87026-8	87026	ae	BZK	BZK	BUL		
91 52 00 87028-4	87028	ae	BZK	DRS	BUL		
91 52 00 87029-2	87029	ae	BZK	BZK	BUL		
91 52 00 87033-4	87033	ae	BZK	BZK	BUL		
91 52 00 87034-2	87034	ae	BZK	BZK	BUL (U)		

Class 92

91 53 0 472 002-1	92001	ae	WGEE	TRA	DBR	ROM	*Mircea Eliad*
91 53 0 472 003-9	92002	ae	WGEE	TRA	DBZ	CRO	*Lucian Blaga*
	92003	ae	WGEE	TRA	EUE	ROM	*Beethoven*
91 53 0 472 005-4	92005	ae	WGEE	TRA	TRA	CRO	
91 53 0 472 001-3	92012	ae	WGEE	TRA	DBR	CRO	
88002	92022	ae	WGEE	DBC	EUE	BUL (U)	*Charles Dickens*
91 53 0 472 004-7	92024	ae	WGEE	TRA	TRB	CRO	*Marin Preda*
91 70 00 92025-1	92025	ae	WGEE	DBC	EUE	BUL	*Oscar Wilde*
	92026	ae	WGEE	TRA	EUE	ROM	*Britten*
91 70 00 92027-7	92027	ae	WGEE	DBC	EUE	BUL	*George Eliot*
91 52 16 88030-1	92030	ae	WGEE	DBC	EUE	BUL	*Ashford*
91 70 00 92034-3	92034	ae	WGEE	DBC	EUE	BUL	*Kipling*
91 53 0 472 006-2	92039	ae	WGEE	TRA	DBR	ROM	*Eugen Ionescu*

3 Preserved locomotives

This section list all the locos classed as preserved, including those that are owned by preservation groups for the supply of spare parts and unlikely to ever be restored. Those locos owned by preservation groups but are main line registered and either on long-term hire to FOCs/TOCs or used for charter work or spot hire are included in section 1. Names are listed even if the plates are not presently fitted because the loco is part way through overhaul. Locos are listed at their home railway unless on a long term loan, but locos do move about and visit other railways or sites.

Loco	previous numbers	key detail differences	livery	location	status	name
Class 01						
D2953	11503	o	GWS	PKR	OP	
D2956	11506	o	BLK	ELR	OP	

Note: Locos do not have train brakes

An enthusiasts' brake van train at Peak Rail is hauled by Class 01 D2953 and Fowler *Bigga* and tailed by Class 02 D2854. *Les Nixon*

Yorkshire Engine Co. Class 02 D2853 stands in front of 03901 and 07012 at Frodingham on 18 April 2015. *Pip Dunn*

Class 02

02003	D2853	vo	GWS	BH	OP
	D2854	vo	GWS	PKR	OP
	D2858	vo	GWS	MRB	UR
	D2860	vo	GWS	NRM	OP
	D2866	vo	BRW	PKR	UR
	D2867	vo	IND	BAT	OP
	D2868	vo	GWS	BH	OP

Class 03

03018	D2018	vo	BRW	MRM	UR
03020	D2020	vo	BRW	MRM	SU
03022	D2022	vo	BRB	SCR	UR
	D2023	vo	GWS	KES	OP
	D2024	vo	IND	KES	SU
03027	D2027	vo	BRW	PKR	UR
03037	D2037	vo	BLK	RDR	SU
	D2041	vo	BLK	CVR	OP
	D2046	vo	IND	PVR	UR
	D2051	vo	GNY	NNR	SU
03059	D2059	xow	GWS	IWR	OP
03062	D2062	xow	GWS	ELR	OP
03063	D2063	xow	BRW	NNR	OP
03066	D2066	xow	BRW	BH	OP
03069	D2069	vo	GWS	VBR	OP
03072	D2072	vo	GWS	LHR	OP
03073	D2073	xow	BRW	RAC	OP
03078	D2078	xow	BLK	NTR	OP

03079	D2079	VO	BRW	DVR	OP	
03081	D2081	VO	BRW	MRM	OP	
03089	D2089	XOW	GWS	MRM	OP	
03090	D2090	VO	GNY	NRS	OP	
03094	D2094	XOW	GWS	RDR	OP	
03099	D2099	VO	BRW	PKR	OP	
03112	D2112	XOW	GWS	RVR	OP	
03113	D2113	VO	BRW	PKR	OP	
	D2117	VO	MAR	LHR	OP	
03118	D2118	VO	BRW	GCN	UR	
03119	D2119	VO	IND	EOR	OP	
03120	D2120	VO	GNY	FHR	OP	
	D2133	VO	GWS	WSR	OP	
03134	D2134	VO	IND	RDR	OP	
	D2138	VO	GWS	MRB	OP	
	D2139	VO	GNY	PKR	OP	
03141	D2141	VO	IND	PBR	UR	
03144	D2144	VO	BRW	WR	OP	
03145	D2145	VO	BRW	MOL	OP	
	D2148	VO	GWS	RSR	UR	
03152	D2152	VO	BRW	SCR	OP	
03158	D2158	XOW	GWS	TIT	OP	*MARGARET-ANN*
03162	D2162	XOW	BRW	LLR	UR	
03170	D2170	XOW	BRW	EOR	OP	
	D2178	VO	GWS	GIR	OP	
03179	D2179	XO	UND	RHR	UR	
03180	D2180	XOW	BRW	PKR	SU	

Formerly BR 03128, this Class 03 has had its original Gardner engine replaced by a 350hp Cummins NT855 engine, hence the decision to number it as an 03/9. *Pip Dunn*

	D2182	vo	GRN	GWR	OP	
	D2184	vo	BLK	CVR	OP	
03189	D2189	vo	BRW	RSR	OP	
	D2192	vo	BLK	PDR	OP	*TITAN*
03197	D2197	xow	BRW	MRM	UR	
	D2199	xow	GWS	PKR	OP	
03371	D2371	xow	BRW	PDR	OP	
03399	D2399	xow	BRW	MRM	OP	
03901	D2128, 03128	xo	BLK	PKR	OP	

Note: 03079/119/120/141/144/145/152/179 have reduced height cabs

Class 04

	D2203	vo	GNY	EBR	OP
	D2205	vo	GSW	PKR	OP
	D2207	vo	GWS	NYM	OP
	D2229	vo	GRE	PR	OP
	D2245	vo	GWS	DVR	OP
	D2246	vo	GWS	SDR	OP
	D2271	vo	GNY	SDR	OP
	D2272	vo	GRE	PKR	UR
	D2279	vo	BLK	PKR	OP
	D2280	vo	BLK	GWR	SU
	D2284	vo	GWS	PR	OP
	D2289	ao	IND	PR	UR
	D2298	vo	GNY	BRC	OP
	D2302	vo	GWS	MOL	UR
04110	D2310	vo	BRW	BAT	OP
	D2324	vo	IND	BU	SU
	D2325	vo	GWS	MRM	OP
	D2334	vo	GWS	MNR	OP
	D2337	vo	GWS	PKR	OP

Class 05

05001	D2554, 97803	vo	GWS	IWR	OP
	D2578	vo	GWS	MOL	OP
	D2587	vo	GWS	PKR	OP
	D2595	vo	GWS	RSR	OP

Class 06

06003	D2420, 97804	vo	GWS	PR	OP

Class 07

07001	D2985	xow	BRW	PKR	OP
07005	D2989	xow	IND	GCR	SU
07010	D2994	vo	BRW	AVR	OP
07012	D2996	vo	BRW	BH	OP
07013	D2997	xow	BRW	ELR	SU

Class 08

	D3000	vo	GNY	PKR	UR	
	D3002	vo	BLK	PVR	OP	
	D3014	vo	BRW	PDR	OP	*SAMSON*

On 20 April 2014, 07012 stands at the platform at the Appleby Frodingham Railway Preservation Society. HNRC's 20066 is in the background. *Pip Dunn*

08011	D3018	vo	GWS	CPR	OP	*HAVERSHAM*
	D3019	vo	UND	CRT	UR	
08015	D3022	vo	GWS	SVR	UR	
08016	D3023	vo	BRW	PKR	OP	
08022	D3030	vo	IND	CWR	OP	*LION*
08032	D3044	vo	BRW	MHR	OP	*MENDIP*
08046	D3059	vo	BRW	CAL	OP	*BRECHIN CITY*
08054	D3067	vo	BRW	EBR	UR	
08060	D3074	vo	IND	CWR	OP	*UNICORN*
08064	D3079	vo	BLK	NRS	UR	
	D3101	vo	GWS	GCR	OP	
08102	D3167	vo	GWS	LWR	OP	
08108	D3174	vo	BLK	KES	SU	*Dover Castle*
08114	D3180	vo	GRE	GCN	OP	
08123	D3190	vo	GRE	CWR	OP	
08133	D3201	vo	GWS	SVR	OP	
08164	D3232	vo	BRW	ELR	OP	*PRUDENCE*
	D3255	vo	UND	MAL	UR	
	D3261	vo	BLK	SCR	OP	
08195	D3265	vo	BLK	LLR	OP	
08202	D3272, 13272	ao	BRW	AVR	OP	
08238	D3308	vo	BRW	DFR	OP	*Charlie*
08266	D3336	vo	DEP	KWV	OP	
08288	D3358	vo	BLK	MHR	OP	
08331	D3401	ao	BLK	MRB	OP	
08359	D3429	vo	BRW	TSR	OP	
08377	D3462	vo	GWS	WSR	OP	
08436	D3551	xo	LSW	SWR	OP	
08443	D3558	vo	GWS	BKR	OP	
08444	D3559	vo	GWS	BWR	OP	
08471	D3586	vo	GWS	SVR	OP	

08473	D3588	vo	BRW	DFR	SU	
08476	D3591	vo	GWS	SWR	OP	
08479	D3594	vo	BLK	ELR	OP	
08490	D3605	vo	BLK	STR	OP	
08495	D3610	xo	BRW	NYM	UR	
08528	D3690	xo	GWS	GCR	OP	
08556	D3723	vo	GWS	NYM	OP	
08590	D3757	xo	BRW	MRB	OP	
08604	D3771	xo	BRW	DRC	OP	*PHANTOM*
08605	D3772	ao	DBS	EVR	OP	*G R Walker*
08633	D3800	ao	EWS	CHV	UR	
08635	D3802	xo	BRW	SVR	UR	
08694	D3861	xo	EWS	GCR	UR	
08767	D3935	xo	GWS	NNR	SU	
08769	D3937	vo	GWS	SVR	OP	*Gladys*
08772	D3940	xo	GWS	NNR	OP	
08773	D3941	xo	BRW	EBR	OP	
08825	D3993	xo	NSO	CPR	OP	
08830	D3998	xow	BLK	PKR	OP	
08850	D4018	xow	BRB	NYM	OP	
08881	D4095	ao	GWS	SDR	OP	
08888	D4118	ao	GWS	KES	UR	
08896	D4126	xo	EWS	SVR	SU	
08907	D4137	ao	GWS	GCR	OP	
08911	D4141	xo	NRM	NRM	OP	*MATEY*
08915	D4145	xo	BRW	NTR	OP	
08922	D4152	ao	EWS	GCN	OP	
08937	D4167	xo	GWS	DAR	OP	*BLUEBELL MEL*
08993	D3759, 08592	xo	EWS	KWV	OP	*ASHBURNHAM*

Note: 08993-995 have reduced bodyheight

08633 has a swinghead coupler

Ex-works after a repaint back into original British Railways green Class 08 D4137 (08907) rests at Loughborough on 13 April 2019. *Pip Dunn*

Class 09

09001	D3665	xow	EWS	PKR	OP	
09004	D3668	xow	BRW	SCR	OP	
09010	D3721	xow	GWS	SDR	OP	
09012	D4100	xow	GWS	SVR	OP	*Dick Hardy*
09015	D4103	xo	EWS	WI	SU	
09017	D4105	xo	NRM	NRM	OP	
09018	D4106	xow	GWS	BLU	OP	
09019	D4107	xow	GWS	WSR	OP	
09024	D4112	xo	DEP	ELR	OP	
09025	D4113	xo	GWS	EKR	OP	
09026	D4114	aow	GWS	SPA	UR	*Cedric Wares*
09107	D4013, 08845	aow	BRW	SVR	OP	

Class 10

	D3452	vo	BLK	BWR	OP	
	D3489	xo	BLK	SPA	UR	*COLONEL TOMLINE*
10119	D4067	vo	BRW	GCR	UR	*Margaret Ethel - Thomas Alfred Naylor*
	D4092	vo	GWS	BH	UR	

Class 11

12052	vo	BLK	CAL	UR	
12077	vo	GWS	MRB	OP	
12082	xo	GWS	MHR	OP	
12083	vo	BLE	BAT	SU	
12088	vo	GWS	ALN	OP	
12093	vo	GWS	CAL	OP	
12099	vo	BLK	SVR	UR	
12131	vo	BLK	NNR	OP	

Note: 12082 carries the number 12049

Class 12

15224	vo	GWS	SPA	OP

Unclassified locos

D2511	vo	GWS	KWV	OP
D2767	vo	GWS	BKR	OP
D2774	vo	GWS	STR	OP
18000	vo	GWR	DRC	SU

PWM/Class 97

97650	PWM650	vo	BRW	PKR	SU
97651	PWM651	vo	GWS	SCR	OP
97654	PWM654	vo	BWS	PR	OP

Class 14

D9500	vo	GWS	PKR	UR
D9502	vo	GWS	ELR	UR
D9504	xo	GWS	KES	OP
D9513	vo	NCB	EBR	OP

Class 14 D9526 leaves Williton with the 1447 Minehead-Bishops Lydeard on 22 June 2019. *Glen Batten*

	D9516	xo	GWS	DRC	OP	
	D9518	vo	NCB	WSR	UR	
	D9520	xo	GWS	NVR	OP	
	D9521	vo	BRW	DFR	OP	
	D9523	xo	MWS	WEN	OP	
14901	D9524	xo	BLU	PKR	UR	
	D9525	vo	GWS	PKR	OP	
	D9526	vo	GWS	WSR	OP	
14029	D9529	xo	BRB	NVR	OP	
	D9531	xo	GWS	ELR	OP	*ERNEST*
	D9537	vo	BLK	ELR	OP	
	D9539	vo	GWS	RSR	OP	
	D9551	vo	GOP	SVR	OP	
	D9553	vo	GWS	WI	UR	
	D9555	vo	GWS	DFR	OP	

Class 15

DB968000	D8233	vo	GYP	ELR	UR

Note: loco has a through steam pipe

Class 17

	D8568	vo	GFY	SVR	OP

Note: Loco has a through steam pipe

Class 17 D8568 passes Hymek D7076 at Hampton Loade as it arrives with the 1347 Kidderminster-Bridgnorth during the Severn Valley Railway's October 2015 diesel gala. *Pip Dunn*

Preserved Class 20s D8137 and D8098 wait to set off with the 1200 Cheltenham Racecourse-Toddington on 29 July 9 2017. *Pip Dunn*

Class 20

20001	D8001	xo	GFY	EOR	OP
20020	D8020	xo	BRB	BKR	UR
20031	D8031	xop	TLC	KWV	OP
20048	D8048	xo	BRB	MRB	UR
20050	D8000	vo	GNY	NRM	SU
20057	D8057	xo	GYP	CHV	SU
20059	D8059	xo	GYP	MHR	OP
20063	D8063	xo	CFD	BAT	UR
20098	D8098	xop	GNY	GCR	OP
20137	D8137	xop	GFY	GWR	UR
20154	D8154	xop	BRB	GCN	OP
20169	D8169	xop	UND	WEN	SU
20188	D8188	xop	GYP	MRB	UR
20214	D8314	xop	GYP	LHR	OP
20228	D8128	xop	BRB	BIR	UR

Note: 20050 has a through steam pipe

Class 23

	D5910	xo	UND	BH	UC

Note: This is a new build loco still under construction. It uses parts of the bodyshell of 37372 (D6859, 37159), which is now regarded as disposed of

One of four surviving Class 24s, 5081 leads Class 26 D5343 into Winchcombe with the 1445 Toddington-Cheltenham Racecourse on 8 October 2016. *Pip Dunn*

Class 24

24032	D5032	vi	GYP	NYM	UR	
24054	D5054, TDB968008	vb	GNY	ELR	OP	*PHIL SOUTHERN*
24061	D5061, RDB968007, 97201	vb	GNY	NYM	UR	
24081	D5081	vo	BRB	GWR	OP	

Class 25

25035	D5185	xip	GYP	GCR	OP	
25059	D5209	xbp	BRB	KWV	OP	
25067	D5217	vb	GYP	BU	SU	
25072	D5222	xi	GRE	CAL	SU	
25083	D5233	vip	BRB	CAL	SU	
25173	D7523	xo	GYP	BAT	UR	
25185	D7535	xo	BRB	SDR	OP	*MERCURY*
25191	D7541	xop	GYP	SDR	UR	
25235	D7585	xip	BRB	BKR	UR	
25244	D7594	xop	UND	KES	SU	
25262	D7612, 25901	xo	GYP	SDR	OP	
25265	D7615	xo	BRB	BU	SU	
25279	D7629	xo	GYP	ELR	OP	
25309	D7659, 25909	xo	GYP	PKR	UR	
25321	D7671	xop	GYP	MRB	UR	
25322	D7672, 25912	xop	BRU	CHV	UR	*TAMWORTH CASTLE*

Class 25s D7612 and D7535 approach Williton with the 1551 Bishops Lydeard-Minehead on 22 June 2019. Both locos were visiting from the South Devon Railway. *Glen Batten*

Class 26

26001	D5301	xo	GNY	CAL	UR	
26002	D5302	xo	GNY	STR	SU	
26004	D5304	xo	TLC	BU	SU	
26007	D5300	xo	RSR	BH	OP	
26010	D5310	xo	GFY	GWR	UR	
26011	D5311	xo	BRB	BU	SU	
26014	D5314	xo	GNY	CAL	OP	
26024	D5324	xop	BRB	BKR	UR	
26025	D5325	xop	GNY	STR	SU	
26035	D5335	xop	BRB	CAL	SU	
26038	D5338	xop	BRB	NYM	OP	*Tom Clift 1954-2012*
26040	D5340	xop	BRB	WAV	UR	
26043	D5343	xop	BRB	GWR	OP	

Class 27

27001	D5347	xip	BRB	BKR	OP
27005	D5351	xbp	BRB	BKR	UR
27007	D5353	vop	UND	CAL	SU
27024	D5370, ADB968028	xop	GYP	CAL	OP
27050	D5394, 27106	xip	GNY	STR	OP
27056	D5401, 27112	xip	GFY	GCR	UR
27059	D5410, 27123, 27205	xotp	UND	LR	UR
27066	D5386, 27103, 27212	xotp	BRB	BH	UR

Class 26 D5343 runs light through Weybourne station on 14 June 2015 while visiting the North Norfolk Railway from the Gloucestershire Warwickshire Railway. *Pip Dunn*

Class 27 D5370 stands at Brechin during the Caledonian Railway's diesel gala on 18 August 2019. *Stuart West*

Class 28

D5705	ADB968006, S15705	vo	GYP	ELR	UR	

Class 31

31018	D5500	vi	BRB	NRM	SU	
31101	D5518	xo	BRB	AVR	OP	
31105	D5523	ao	NRY	MRM	OP	
31106	D5524	xo	BRB	WR	OP	Spalding Town
31108	D5526	xop	RFO	MRB	OP	
31119	D5537	xo	BRB	EBR	SU	
31130	D5548	xop	RFO	AVR	UR	
31162	D5580	xi	BRB	MRB	OP	
31190	D5613	xo	GOP	WR	OP	
31203	D5627	xo	GNY	PBR	OP	Steve Ogden GM
31206	D5630	xo	CCE	RHR	UR	
31207	D5631	xo	GNY	NNR	UR	
31210	D5634	xop	RFO	DFR	UR	
31233	D5553	ao	NRY	MRM	OP	
31235	D5662	xo	BRB	DFR	UR	
31255	D5683	xo	EWS	MNR	UR	
31270	D5800	xop	REG	PKR	SU	Athena
31271	D5801	xop	TLA	LR	OP	Stratford 1840-2001
31285	D5817	ao	NRY	WR	OP	
31289	D5821	xo	EBP	RHR	OP	PHŒNIX
31327	D5862	xo	GYP	STR	OP	
31414	D5814	xe	GYP	MRB	UR	
31418	D5522	xei	BRB	MRB	UR	
31430	D5695, 31265, 31530	xy	BRB	SPA	OP	Sister Dora
31435	D5600, 31179	xe	GYE	EBR	SU	
31438	D5557, 31139, 31538	xe	BRB	EOR	OP	
31452	D5809, 31279, 31552	xe	DCG	DAR	OP	
31463	D5830, 31297, 31563	xe	GOP	GCN	OP	
31465	D5637, 31213, 31565	ae	NRY	WR	OP	
31466	D5533, 31115	xep	EWS	DFR	OP	
31601	D5609, 31186	xozf	DCR	EVR	OP	Devon Diesel Society
97205	D5581, 31163	xo	RTC	CPR	OP	

Class 33

33002	D6501	xyp	GYP	SDR	OP	
33008	D6508	xyp	GYP	BAT	UR	Eastleigh
33018	D6530	xyp	BRB	MRM	UR	
33019	D6534	xyp	DUT	BAT	UR	Griffon
33021	D6539	xyp	POR	CHV	OP	Eastleigh
33035	D6553	xyp	BRB	ELR	OP	
33046	D6564	xyp	SWT	ELR	SU	
33048	D6566	xyp	GYP	WSR	OP	
33052	D6570	xyp	GNY	KES	SU	Ashford
33053	D6571	xyp	BRB	MHR	OP	
33057	D6575	xep	GYP	WSR	OP	

Preserved 31163 has been renumbered 97205 and repainted into the Research livery of the Railway Technical Centre once carried by 97204. On 4 May 2018, the loco was a visitor to the Keighley and Worth Valley Railway gala. *Stuart West*

33202 stands at Dereham during a visit to the Mid Norfolk Railway for its diesel gala on 6 April 2019. *Stuart West*

33063	D6583	xep	TMF	SPA	OP	*RJ Mitchell – DESIGNER OF THE SPITFIRE*
33065	D6585	xep	BRB	SPA	UR	*Sealion*
33102	D6513	xew	BRB	CHV	OP	*Sophie*
33103	D6514	xewp	DEP	EVR	OP	*SWORDFISH*
33108	D6521	xew	BRB	SVR	OP	
33109	D6525	xew	DEP	ELR	OP	*Captain Bill Smith RNR*
33110	D6527	xew	DEP	BWR	OP	
33111	D6528	xew	BRB	SWR	OP	
33116	D6535	xewp	BRB	GCR	OP	
33117	D6536	xew	BRB	ELR	SU	
33201	D6586	xesp	BRB	EOR	OP	
33202	D6587	xesp	BRB	MRM	OP	*Dennis G. Robinson*
33208	D6593	xesp	GYP	BAT	SU	

Class 35

	D7017	vop	GYP	WSR	OP
	D7018	vop	GYP	WSR	OP
	D7029	vop	BRB	SVR	UR
	D7076	vbp	BRB	ELR	UR

Class 37

37003	D6703	xot	BRB	LR	UR
37009	D6709, 37340	xot	BRB	GCR	UR
37023	D6723	xo	UND	ALL	UR
37029	D6729	xot	GYP	EOR	OP
37032	D6732, 37353	xot	GYP	NNR	OP

Returned to traffic in 2019 after a 25-year overhaul, Hymek D7018 approaches Blue Anchor with the 1059 from Minehead on 21 June 2019. *Glen Batten*

37037	D6737, 37321	xip	BRB	SDR	UR	
37042	D6742	xot	EWS	EDR	SU	
37075	D6775	xop	TTG	KWV	OP	
37097	D6797	xo	BRB	CAL	UR	*Old Fettercairn*
37108	D6808, 37325	xip	BRB	RAC	UR	
37109	D6809	xo	BRB	ELR	OP	
37142	D6842	xop	BRB	BWR	OP	
37214	D6914	xot	WCR	BKR	SU	
37215	D6915	xotp	BRB	GWR	UR	
37216	D6916	xotp	GYP	PBR	UR	
37227	D6927	xotp	TLM	CPR	OP	
37248	D6948	xotp	GYP	GWR	OP	
37250	D6950	xotp	DCE	WEN	OP	
37261	D6961	aip	DRU	BKR	UR	
37263	D6963	xop	BRB	TSR	UR	
37264	D6964	xip	LLB	NYM	OP	
37275	D6975	xotp	BRB	PDR	OP	
37294	D6994	xotp	BRB	EBR	OP	
37308	D6608, 37274	xotp	UND	DFR	UR	
37310	D6852, 37152	xop	BRB	PKR	UR	*British Steel Ravenscraig*
37350	D6700, 37119	xot	GYP	NRM	SU	
37503	D6717, 37017	aotp	EWS	WEN	SU	
37674	D6869, 37169	xotp	RSR	WEN	OP	
37679	D6823, 37123	xotp	TTG	ELR	SU	
37688	D6905, 37205	xotp	TLA	SVR	OP	*Great Rocks*
37703	D6767, 37067	xotp	DRU	BKR	OP	
37714	D6724, 37024	xotp	TLM	GCR	OP	*Cardiff Canton*

Class 37 D6948 pauses at Gotherington with the 0930 Toddington-Cheltenham Racecourse on 29 July 2017.
Pip Dunn

No. 40106 *Atlantic Conveyor* leaves Arley with the 1259 Kidderminster-Bridgnorth on 16 May 2019.
Glen Batten

Class 40

40012	D212, 97407	xi	BRB	ELR	UR	*AUREOL*
40106	D306	vb	GFY	ELR	OP	*ATLANTIC CONVEYOR*
40118	D318, 97408	xi	BRB	TRM	UR	
40122	D200	xi	GNY	NRM	SU	
40135	D335, 97406	xb	BRB	ELR	UR	

Class 41

41001	43000, ADB975812	ae	BRP	NH	UR	

Class 42

	D821	vi	MYP	SVR	OP	*GREYHOUND*
	D832	vb	GYP	ELR	OP	*ONSLAUGHT*

Class 43

43002		ae	HST	NRM	SU

Class 44

44004	D4	vo	BRB	MRB	UR	*GREAT GABLE*
44008	D8	vo	GYP	PKR	OP	*PENYGHENT*

Just one of two surviving Class 42 Warships, D821 *Greyhound* exits Bewdley Tunnel with the 1110 to Bridgnorth on 19 May 2019. *Glen Batten*

The first production series HST power car 43002 *Sir Kenneth Grange* has been claimed for display as part of the National Collection. On March 7 2019, in its final couple of months in traffic, it pauses at Westbury on the rear of 1A77, the 0505 Penzance-Paddington. *Mark Pike*

D123 *Leicestershire and Derbyshire Yeomanry* runs light to Loughborough shed having arrived with the 1118 from Rothley on 7 September 2019. *Pip Dunn*

Class 45

45015	D14	xo	BRB	BAT	SU	
45041	D53	xi	BRB	NVR	OP	*ROYAL TANK REGIMENT*
45060	D100	xi	BRB	BH	UR	*SHERWOOD FORESTER*
45105	D86	xe	BRB	BH	UR	
45108	D120	xe	BRB	ELR	OP	
45112	D61	xe	BRB	BU	SU	*ROYAL ARMY ORDNACE CORPS*
45125	D123	xe	GYP	GCR	OP	*LEICESTERSHIRE AND DERBYSHIRE YEOMANRY*
45132	D22	xe	BRB	EOR	UR	
45133	D40	xe	BRB	MRB	UR	
45135	D99	xe	BRB	ELR	UR	*3rd CARABINIER*
45149	D135	xe	BRB	GWR	OP	

Class 46

46010	D147	xo	BRB	GCN	OP	
46035	D172, 97403	xo	BRB	PKR	SU	
46045	D182, 97404	xb	BYP	MRB	UR	

Class 47

47004	D1524	xip	GYP	EBR	SU	
47077	D1661, 47613, 47840	xyt	BRB	WSR	UR	*NORTH STAR*
47105	D1693	xb	BRB	GWR	UR	

47117	D1705	xip	BRB	GCR	OP	*SPARROWHAWK*
47192	D1842	xo	GFY	RAC	OP	
47205	D1855, 47395	aotm	RFD	NLR	OP	
47292	D1994	xotm	BLL	GCN	OP	
47306	D1787	xotm	RFE	BWR	OP	*The Sapper*
47367	D1886	xos	BRB	MNR	OP	*KENNY COCKBIRD*
47376	D1895	xos	FTT	GWR	OP	*Freightliner 1995*
47401	D1500	xe	BRB	MRB	OP	*North Eastern*
47402	D1501	xe	GYP	ELR	OP	
47417	D1516	xei	GYP	MRB	UR	
47449	D1566	xe	BRB	LLR	OP	
47484	D1662	xe	GWR	WIS	UR	*ISAMBARD KINGDOM BRUNEL*
47579	D1778, 47183, 47793	xet	BRE	MHR	OP	*James Nightall GC*
47596	D1933, 47255	xe	NSD	MNR	OP	*Aldeburgh Festival*
47635	D1606, 47029	xe	LLB	EOR	OP	*Jimmy Milne*
47640	D1921, 47244	xe	LLB	BAT	OP	*University of Strathclyde*
47643	D1970, 47269	xep	IOS	BKR	OP	
47761	D1619, 47038, 47564	aet	RES	MRB	SU	
47765	D1643, 47059, 47631	xet	SCR	ELR	OP	
47771	D1946, 47503	aet	RES	ZG	SU	
47785	D1909, 47232, 47665, 47820	xet	EWS	WEN	SU	
47799	D1654, 47070, 47620, 47835	aet	ROY	EDR	SU	*Prince Henry*

On 29 July 2017, 47376 arrives at Winchcombe with the 1350 Toddington-Cheltenham Racecourse. *Pip Dunn*

Recently a main line certified loco, 50017 *Royal Oak* has now been sold for preservation and is based at the Great Central Railway. It runs round at Leicester North, having arrived with the 1200 from Loughborough on 13 April 2019. *Pip Dunn*

Class 50

50002	D402	xep	BRB	SDR	UR	
50015	D415	xep	LLB	ELR	OP	*Valiant*
50017	D417	xep	NSO	GCR	OP	*Royal Oak*
50019	D419	xep	LLB	MNR	UR	*Ramillies*
50021	D421	xep	LLB	ZG	UR	*Rodney*
50026	D426	xep	NSD	ZG	UR	*Indomitable*
50027	D427	xep	NSR	MHR	UR	*Lion*
50029	D429	xep	LLB	PKR	SU	*Renown*
50030	D430	xep	LLB	PKR	UR	*Repulse*
50031	D431	xep	ICS	SVR	UR	*Hood*
50033	D433	xep	LLB	SVR	OP	*Glorious*
50035	D435	xep	BRB	SVR	OP	*Ark Royal*
50042	D442	xep	LLB	BWR	OP	*Triumph*

Class 52

	D1010	xo	MYP	WSR	UR	*WESTERN CAMPAIGNER*
	D1013	xo	BRB	SVR	UR	*WESTERN RANGER*
	D1023	xi	BRB	NRM	SU	*WESTERN FUSILIER*
	D1041	xo	BRB	ELR	UR	*WESTERN PRINCE*
	D1048	xo	BRB	MRB	UR	*WESTERN LADY*
	D1062	xo	BRB	SVR	OP	*WESTERN COURIER*

Class 55

55015	D9015	xe	GYP	BH	UR	*TULYAR*
55019	D9019	xe	BRB	BH	OP	*ROYAL HIGHLAND FUSILIER*

Class 56

56006		aos	BRB	ELR	OP	
56097		aos	TLC	GCN	OP	

Class 58

58012		aosp	TMF	BAT	SU
58016		aosp	FER	LR	UR
58022		aosp	TMF	PKR	SU
58023		aosp	MLB	BAT	UR
58048		aosp	EWS	BAT	SU

Main line electric locos

Last number	Previous official numbers carried	Key detail differences	Livery	Location	Status	Current name
Class 71						
71001	E5001	xe	UND	NRS	UR	
Class 73						
73003	E6003	xew	GYP	SCR	OP	*Sir Herbert Walker*
73114	E6020	xew	UND	BU	UR	
73118	E6024	xewl	EUS	BIR	OP	
73129	E6036	xew	EBP	GWR	OP	
73130	E6037	xewl	EUS	FIN	OP	
73140	E6047	xew	NSR	SPA	OP	
73210	E6022, 73116	xew	IGX	EVR	OP	*Selhurst*
Class 76						
76020	E26020	vo	BLK	NRM	SU	
Class 77						
1502	E27000	ae	BLK	MRB	SU	*ELECTRA*
1505	E27001	ae	DNS	MSIM	SU	*ARIADNE*
1501	E27003	ae	DNS	TIL	OP	*DIANA*
Class 81						
81002	E3003	xe	BRB	BH	SU	
Class 82						
82008	E3054	xe	ICO	BH	SU	
Class 83						
83012	E3035	xe	EBY	BH	SU	
Class 84						
84001	E3036	xe	BRB	BKR	SU	

Class 85

| 85006 | E3061, 85101 | xe | | BRB | BH | SU | |

Class 87

| 87001 | | ae | | BRB | NRM | SU | *Stephenson* |
| 87035 | | ae | | BRB | RAC | UR | *Robert Burns* |

Class 89

| 89001 | | ae | | ICO | BH | UR | |

Prototype Type 5 diesel-electric Co-Co

| DP1 | | vi | | POW | NRS | SU | *DELTIC* |

Note: The number DP1 was not displayed on the locomotive

Prototype 500hp diesel-electric 0-6-0

| D226 | D0226 | vo | | GRE | KWV | OP | |

Initially preserved by the AC Locomotive Group, 87002 *Royal Sovereign* has been main line registered for several years now and a hire contract with GB Railfreight has seen it repainted into Caledonian Sleeper livery. On 9 January 2019, the loco passes Peterborough running as 0Z87, the 0933 Wembley-Doncaster Down Decoy Yard. *Stuart West*

4 Disposed locomotives

This part lists all locos that were owned or leased by BR and subsequent private TOCs/FOCs but have since been scrapped. They are listed by their last number carried, and all previous numbers are detailed, with the most recent number(s) applied before the last number. Some locos, such as Class 31/5s and 47/8s, carried the same TOPS number twice. Locos owned by the 'Big four' that were withdrawn before nationalisation are not included. All pre-TOPS numbers on diesels were initially prefixed D, which may or may not have been removed and so are excluded. Any allocated TOPS numbers that were allocated or intended, but not applied are not listed. Industrial shunting locos registered in the 015xx series are not detailed.

Unclassified LMS shunters

	7055
	7056
7408	7058

Unclassified shunter diesel-mechanical 0-4-0

2400	11177
2401	11178
2402	11179
2403	11180
2404	11181
2405	11182
2406	11183
2407	11184
2408	11185
2409	11186

Unclassified shunter diesel-mechanical 0-4-0

2500	11116
2501	11117
2502	11118
2503	11119
2504	11120
2505	11144
2506	11145
2507	11146
2508	11147
2509	11148
2510	
2512	
2513	
2514	
2515	
2516	
2517	
2518	
2519	

Unclassified shunter diesel-hydraulic 0-4-0

2700	11700
2701	11701
2702	11702
2703	11703
2704	11704
2705	11705
2706	11706
2707	11707

Unclassified shunter diesel-hydraulic 0-4-0

2708	11708
2709	11709
2710	11710
2711	11711
2712	11712
2713	11713
2714	11714
2715	11715
2716	11716
2717	11717
2718	11718
2719	11719
2720	
2721	
2722	
2723	
2724	

2725
2726
2727
2728
2729
2730
2731
2732
2733
2734
2735
2736
2737
2738
2739
2740
2741
2742
2743
2744
2745
2746
2747
2748
2749
2750
2751
2752
2753
2754
2755
2756
2757
2758
2759
2760
2761
2762
2763
2764
2765
2766
2768
2769
2770
2771
2772
2773
2775
2776
2777
2778
2779
2780

Unclassified shunter diesel-hydraulic 0-4-0

2900
2901
2902
2903
2904
2905
2906
2907
2908

2909	
2910	
2911	
2912	
2913	

Unclassified shunter diesel mechanical 0-4-0
2950	11500
2951	11501
2952	11502

Unclassified shunter diesel-mechanical 0-4-0
2957	11507
2958	11508

Unclassified shunter diesel-electric 0-4-0
2999

Unclassified shunter diesel-electric 0-6-0
3117	13117
3118	13118
3119	13119
3120	13120
3121	13121
3122	13122
3123	13123
3124	13124
3125	13125
3126	13126
3152	1352
3153	1353
3154	1354
3155	1355
3156	1356
3157	1357
3158	1358
3159	1359
3160	1360
3161	1361
3162	1362
3163	1363
3164	1364
3165	1365
3166	1366

Unclassified shunter diesel-mechanical 0-6-0
11104

This was the same design as a Class 04

Unclassified shunter diesel-electric 0-6-0
12000
12001

Unclassified shunter diesel-electric 0-6-0
12002

Unclassified shunter diesel-electric 0-6-0
12003	7080
12004	7081
12005	7082
12006	7083
12007	7084
12008	7085
12009	7086
12010	7087
12011	7088
12012	7089
12013	7090
12014	7091
12015	7092
12016	7093
12017	7094
12018	7095
12019	7096
12020	7097
12021	7098
12022	7099
12023	7110
12024	7111
12025	7112
12026	7113
12027	7114
12028	7115
12029	7116
12030	7117
12031	7118
12032	7119

LNER Unclassified shunter diesel-electric 0-6-0
15000	8000
15001	8001
15002	8002
15003	8003

LNER Unclassified shunter diesel-electric 0-6-0
15004

GWR Unclassified shunter diesel-electric 0-6-0
15100

GWR Unclassified shunter diesel-electric 0-6-0
15101
15102
15103
15104
15105
15106

Unclassified shunter diesel-electric 0-6-0
15107

SR Unclassified shunter diesel-electric 0-6-0
15201
15202
15203

LMS Prototype Type 3 1,600hp diesel-electric Co-Co
10000
10001

Prototype 2,040hp diesel-mechanical 2-D-2
10100

Prototype Type 3 1,750hp diesel-electric 1Co-Co1
10201
10202

Prototype Type 4 2,000hp diesel-electric 1Co-Co1
10203

Prototype Type 1 827hp diesel-electric Bo-Bo
10800

Prototype 500hp Diesel-mechanical 0-6-0
11001

Prototype 500hp diesel-hydraulic 0-6-0
D227	D0227

Prototype Type 4 diesel-electric Co-Co
DP2

Prototype Type 4 diesel-electric Co-Co
0260

Prototype Type 5 diesel-electric Co-Co
HS4000

Various trial locos
D9998
JANUS
TAURUS
VULCAN

Unclassified electric Bo-Bo
26500	6480
26501	6481

Unclassified electric Bo-Bo
26502	6490
26503	6491
26504	6492
26505	6493
26506	6494
26507	6495
26508	6496
26509	6497
26510	6498
26511	6499

Unclassified electric Bo-Bo
26600	6999

Unlassified gas turbine A1A-A1A
E1000	E2000	18100

Unclassified gas turbine 4-6-0

GT3

Class 01 shunter diesel-mechanical 0-4-0

01001	2954	11504
01002	2955	11505
	2956	

Two locos were numbered D2956: this one and the Class 01 that is preserved

Class 02 shunter diesel-hydraulic 0-4-0

02001	2850
	2851
	2852
	2855
02004	2856
	2857
	2859
	2861
	2862
	2863
	2864
	2865
	2869

Class 03 shunter diesel-mechanical 0-6-0

	2000		03075	2075
	2001		03076	2076
	2002			2074
	2003			2077
03004	2004		03080	2080
03005	2005			2082
	2006			2083
03007	2007			2085
03008	2008		03086	2086
03009	2009			2087
03010	2010			2088
	2011		03091	2091
03012	2012		03092	2092
03013	2013			2093
03014	2014		03095	2095
	2015		03096	2096
03016	2016		03097	2097
03017	2017		03098	2098
	2019			2100
03021	2021			2101
03025	2025		03102	2102
03026	2026		03103	2103
	2028		03104	2104
03029	2029		03105	2105
	2030		03106	2106
	2031		03107	2107
	2032		03108	2108
	2033		03109	2109
03034	2034		03110	2110
03035	2035		03111	2111
	2036			2114
	2038			2115
	2039			2116
	2040		03121	2121
	2042			2122
	2043			2123
03044	2044			2124
03045	2045			2125
03047	2047			2126
	2048			2127
	2049		03129	2129
03050	2050			2130
	2052			2131
	2053			2132
	2054		03135	2135
03055	2055			2136
03056	2056		03137	2137
	2057			2140
03058	2058		03142	2142
03060	2060			2143
03061	2061			2146
03064	2064		03147	2147
	2065		03149	2149
03067	2067			2150
03068	2068		03151	2151
	2070		03153	2153
	2071		03154	2154
			03155	2155
			03157	2157
			03159	2159
			03160	2160
			03161	2161
			03163	2163
			03164	2164
			03165	2165
			03166	2166
			03167	2167
			03168	2168
			03169	2169
			03171	2171
			03172	2172
				2173
			03174	2174
			03175	2175
				2176
				2177
				2181
				2183
				2185
				2186
				2187
				2188
				2190

	2191
	2193
	2194
	2195
	2198
03370	2370
	2372
	2373
	2374
	2375
	2376
	2377
	2378
	2379
	2380
03382	2382
	2383
	2384
	2385
03386	2386
	2387
	2388
03389	2389
	2390
	2391
	2392
	2393
	2394
	2395
	2396
03397	2397
	2398

Class 04 shunter diesel-mechanical 0-6-0

2200	11100	2255	11225
2201	11101	2256	11226
2202	11102	2257	11227
2204	11105	2258	11228
2206	11107	2259	11229
2208	11109	2260	
2209	11110	2261	
2210	11111	2262	
2211	11112	2263	
2212	11113	2264	
2213	11114	2265	
2214	11115	2266	
2215	11121	2267	
2216	11122	2268	
2217	11123	2269	
2218	11124	2270	
2219	11125	2273	
2220	11126	2274	
2221	11127	2275	
2222	11128	2276	
2223	11129	2277	
2224	11130	2278	
2225	11131	2281	
2226	11132	2282	
2227	11133	2283	
2228	11134	2285	
2230	11149	2286	
2231	11150	2287	
2232	11151	2288	
2233	11152	2290	
2234	11153	2291	
2235	11154	2292	
2236	11155	2293	
2237	11156	2294	
2238	11157	2295	
2239	11158	2296	
2240	11159	2297	
2241	11160	2298	
2242	11212	2299	
2243	11213	2300	
2244	11214	2301	
2247	11217	2303	
2248	11218	2304	
2249	11219	2305	
2250	11220	2306	
2251	11221	2307	
2252	11222	2308	
2253	11223	2309	
2254	11224	2311	
		2312	
		2313	
		2314	
		2315	
		2316	
		2317	
		2318	
		2319	
		2320	
		2321	
		2322	
		2323	
		2326	
		2327	
		2328	
		2329	
		2330	
		2331	
		2332	
		2333	
		2335	
		2336	
		2338	
		2339	
		2340	
		2341	S1173

Class 05 shunter diesel-mechanical 0-6-0

2550	11136
2551	11137
2552	11138
2553	11139
2555	11141
2556	11142

2557	11143
2558	11161
2559	11162
2560	11163
2561	11164
2562	11165
2563	11166
2564	11167
2565	11168
2566	11169
2567	11170
2568	11171
2569	11172
2570	11173
2571	11174
2572	11175
2573	11176
2574	
2575	
2576	
2577	
2579	
2580	
2581	
2582	
2583	
2584	
2585	
2586	
2588	
2589	
2590	
2591	
2592	
2593	
2594	
2596	
2597	
2598	
2599	
2600	
2601	
2602	
2603	
2604	
2605	
2606	
2607	
2608	
2609	
2610	
2611	
2612	
2613	
2614	
2615	
2616	
2617	
2618	

Class 06 shunter diesel-mechanical 0-4-0

	2410
	2411
	2412
06001	2413
06002	2414
	2415
	2416
	2417
	2418
	2419
06004	2421
06005	2422
06006	2423
	2424
	2425
06007	2426
	2427
	2428
	2429
	2430
	2431
	2432

	2433
	2434
	2435
	2436
06008	2437
	2438
	2439
06009	2440
	2441
	2442
	2443
06010	2444

Class 07 shunter diesel-electric 0-6-0

07002	2986
07003	2987
	2988
07006	2990
	2992
07009	2993
	2998

Class 08 shunter diesel-electric 0-6-0

	3001	13001
	3003	13003
08001	3004	13004
08002	3005	13005
ADB966507	3006	13006
08003	3007	13007
08004	3008	13008
08005	3009	13009
08006	3010	13010
	3011	13011
	3012	13012
	3013	13013
08008	3015	13015
08009	3016	13016
08010	3017	13017
	3020	13020
08014	3021	13021
	3024	13024
08018	3025	13025
	3026	13026
08019	3027	13027
	3028	13028
08023	3031	13031
08024	3032	13032
08025	3033	13033
	3034	13034
ADB966508	3035	13035
08026	3036	13036
ADB966510	3037	13037
	3038	13038
08027	3039	13039
08028	3040	13040
08029	3041	13041
08030	3042	13042
08031	3043	13043
	3045	13045
08033	3046	13046
08035	3048	13048
08036	3049	13049
08037	3050	13050
	3051	13051
	3052	13052
	3053	13053
08041	3054	13054
08042	3055	13055
08043	3056	13056
08044	3057	13057
08045	3058	13058
08047	3060	13060
08048	3061	13061
08049	3062	13062
08050	3063	13063
08051	3064	13064
08052	3065	13065
08053	3066	13066
08055	3068	13068
ADB966509	3069	13069
08056	3070	13070
08057	3071	13071
08058	3072	13072

08xxx	3xxx	13xxx	
08059	3073	13073	
08061	3075	13075	
08062	3076	13076	
08063	3077	13077	
ADB966506	3078	13078	
08065	3080	13080	
08066	3081	13081	
08067	3082	13082	
08068	3083	13083	
08069	3084	13084	
08070	3085	13085	
08071	3086	13086	
	3087	13087	
	3088	13088	
08074	3089	13089	
08075	3090	13090	
08076	3091	13091	
	3093	13093	
	3094	13094	
	3095	13095	
	3096	13096	
	3097	13097	
	3098	13098	
	3099	13099	
	3100	13100	
08077	3102	13102	
08078	3103	13103	
08079	3104	13104	
08080	3105	13105	
08081	3106	13106	
08082	3107	13107	
08083	3108	13108	
08084	3109	13109	
08085	3110	13110	
08086	3111	13111	
08087	3112	13112	
08088	3113	13113	
08089	3114	13114	
08090	3115	13115	
08091	3116	13116	
08092	3127	13127	
08093	3128	13128	
08094	3129	13129	
08095	3130	13130	
08096	3131	13131	
08097	3132	13132	
08098	3133	13133	
08099	3134	13134	
08100	3135	13135	
08101	3136	13136	
08103	3168	13168	
08104	3169	13169	
08105	3170	13170	
08106	3171	13171	
	3172	13172	
08107	3173	13173	
08109	3175	13175	
08110	3176	13176	
08111	3177	13177	ADB966512
08112	3178	13178	
08113	3179	13179	
08115	3181	13181	
08116	3182	13182	
	3183	13183	
08117	3184	13184	ADB966513
08118	3185	13185	
08119	3186	13186	ADB966511
08120	3187	13187	
08121	3188	13188	
08122	3189	13189	
08124	3191	13191	
08125	3192	13192	
	3193	13193	
08126	3194	13194	
08127	3195	13195	
08128	3196	13196	
08129	3197	13197	
08130	3198	13198	
08131	3199	13199	
08132	3200	13200	
08134	3202	13202	
08135	3203	13203	
08136	3204	13204	

08xxx	3xxx	13xxx	
08137	3205	13205	
08138	3206	13206	
08139	3207	13207	
08140	3208	13208	
08141	3209	13209	
08142	3210	13210	
08143	3211	13211	
08144	3212	13212	
08145	3213	13213	
08146	3214	13214	
08147	3215	13215	
08148	3216	13216	
08149	3217	13217	
08150	3218	13218	
08151	3219	13219	
08152	3220	13220	
08153	3221	13221	
08154	3222	13222	
08155	3223	13223	
08156	3224	13224	
08157	3225	13225	
08158	3226	13226	
08159	3227	13227	
08160	3228	13228	
08161	3229	13229	
08162	3230	13230	
08163	3231	13231	
08165	3233	13233	
08166	3234	13234	
08167	3235	13235	
08169	3237	13237	
08170	3238	13238	
08171	3239	13239	
08172	3240	13240	
08173	3241	13241	PO1
08174	3242	13242	
08175	3243	13243	
08176	3244	13244	
08177	3245	13245	
08178	3246	13246	
08179	3247	13247	
08180	3248	13248	
08181	3249	13249	
08182	3250	13250	
08183	3251	13251	
08184	3252	13252	
08185	3253	13253	
08186	3254	13254	
08187	3256	13256	
08188	3257	13257	
08189	3258	13258	
08190	3259	13259	
08191	3260	13260	
08192	3262	13262	
08193	3263	13263	
08194	3264	13264	
08196	3266	13266	
08197	3267	13267	
08198	3268	13268	
08199	3269	13269	
08200	3270	13270	
08201	3271	13271	
08204	3274	13274	
08205	3275	13275	
08206	3276	13276	
08207	3277	13277	
08208	3278	13278	
08209	3279	13279	
08210	3280	13280	
08211	3281	13281	
08212	3282	13282	
08213	3283	13283	
08214	3284	13284	
08215	3285	13285	
08216	3286	13286	
08217	3287	13287	
08218	3288	13288	
08219	3289	13289	
08221	3291	13291	
08222	3292	13292	
08223	3293	13293	
08224	3294	13294	
08225	3295	13295	

08226	3296	13296	08313	3383
08227	3297	13297	08314	3384
08228	3298	13298	08315	3385
08229	3299	13299	08316	3386
08230	3300	13300	08317	3387
08231	3301	13301	08318	3388
08232	3302	13302	08319	3389
08233	3303	13303	08320	3390
08234	3304	13304	08321	3391
08235	3305	13305	08322	3392
08236	3306	13306	08323	3393
08237	3307	13307	08324	3394
08239	3309	13309	08325	3395
08240	3310	13310	08326	3396
08241	3311	13311	08327	3397
08242	3312	13312	08328	3398
08243	3313	13313	08329	3399
08244	3314	13314	08330	3400
08245	3315	13315	08332	3402
08246	3316	13316	08333	3403
08247	3317	13317 PO1	08334	3404
08248	3318	13318	08335	3405
08249	3319	13319	08336	3406
08250	3320	13320	08337	3407
08251	3321	13321	08338	3408
08252	3322	13322	08339	3409
08253	3323	13323	08340	3410
08254	3324	13324	08341	3411
08255	3325	13325	08342	3412
08256	3326	13326	08343	3413
08257	3327	13327	08344	3414
08258	3328	13328	08345	3415
08260	3330	13330	08346	3416
08261	3331	13331	08347	3417
08262	3332	13332	08348	3418
08263	3333	13333	08349	3419
08264	3334	13334	08350	3420
08265	3335	13335	08351	3421
08267	97801	RDB968020	08352	3422
	3337	13337	08353	3423
08268	3338	13338	08354	3424
08269	3339	13339	08355	3425
08270	3340	13340	08356	3426
08271	3341	13341	08357	3427
08272	3342	13342	08358	3428
08273	3343	13343	08360	3430
08274	3344	13344	08361	3431
08275	3345	13345	08362	3432
08276	3346	13346	08363	3433
08277	3347	13347	08364	3434
08278	3348	13348	08365	3435
08279	3349	13349	08366	3436
08280	3350	13350	08367	3437
08281	3351	13351	08368	3438
08282	3352	13352	08369	3454
08283	3353	13353	08370	3455
08284	3354	13354	08371	3456
08285	3355	13355	08372	3457
08286	3356	13356	08373	3458
08287	3357	13357	08374	3459
08289	3359		08376	3461
08290	3360		08378	3463
08291	3361		08379	3464
08292	3362	13362	08380	3465
08293	3363	13363	08381	3466
08294	3364	13364	08382	3467
08295	3365	13365	08383	3468
08296	3366	13366	08384	3469
08297	3367		08385	3470
08298	3368		08386	3471
08299	3369		08387	3472
08300	3370		08388	3503
08301	3371		08390	3505
08302	3372		08391	3506
08303	3373		08392	3507
08304	3374		08393	3508
08305	3375		08394	3509
08306	3376		08395	3510
08307	3377		08396	3511
08309	3379		08397	3512
08310	3380		08398	3513
08311	3381		08399	3514
08312	3382		08400	3515

08402	3517	08522	3684
08403	3518	08524	3686
08404	3519	08526	3688
08406	3521	08529	3691
08407	3522	08532	3694
08408	3523	08533	3695
08409	3524	08534	3696
08412	3527	08535	3699
08413	3528	08537	3701
08414	3529	08538	3702
08415	3530	08539	3703
08416	3531	08540	3704
08419	3534	08541	3705
08420	3535	08542	3706
08422	3537	08543	3707
08424	3539	08544	3708
08425	3540	08545	3709
08426	3541	08546	3710
08427	3542	08547	3711
08429	3544	08548	3712
08430	3545	08549	3713
08431	3546	08550	3714
08432	3547	08551	3715
08433	3548	08552	3716
08434	3549	08553	3717
08435	3550	08554	3718
08437	3552	08555	3722
08438	3553	08557	3724
08439	3554	08558	3725
08440	3555	08559	3726
08446	3561	08560	3727
08448	3563	08561	3728
08449	3564	08562	3729
08450	3565	08563	3730
08452	3567	08564	3731
08453	3568	08565	3732
08455	3570	08566	3733
08456	3571	08569	3736
08457	3572	08570	3737
08458	3573	08572	3739
08459	3574	08574	3741
08461	3576	08576	3743
08463	3578	08577	3744
08464	3579	08579	3746
08465	3580	08581	3748
08466	3581	08582	3749
08467	3582	08583	3750
08468	3583	08584	3751
08469	3584	08586	3753
08470	3585	08587	3754
08474	3589	08589	3756
08475	3590	08591	3758
08477	3592	08594	3761
08478	3593	08595	3762
08481	3596	08597	3764
08482	3597	08599	3766
08486	3601	08601	3768
08487	3602	08603	3770
08488	3603	08606	3773
08489	3604	08607	3774
08491	3606	08608	3775
08492	3607	08609	3776
08493	3608	08610	3777
08494	3609	08612	3779
08496	3611	08614	3781
08497	3652	08618	3785
08498	3653	08619	3786
08501	3656	08621	3788
08504	3659	08625	3792
08505	3660	08626	3793
08506	3661	08627	3794
08508	3663	08628	3795
08509	3664	08634	3801
08510	3672	08636	3803
08512	3674	08637	3805
08513	3675	08638	3805
08514	3676	08639	3806
08515	3677	08640	3807
08517	3679	08642	3809
08518	3680	08646	3813
08519	3681	08647	3814
08520	3682	08651	3818
08521	3683	08654	3821

08655	3822	08793	3961
08656	3823	08794	3962
08657	3824	08796	3964
08658	3825	08797	3965
08659	3826	08800	3968
08660	3827	08801	3969
08661	3828	08803	3971
08662	3829	08806	3974
08664	3831	08807	3975
08665	3832	08808	3976
08666	3833	08811	3979
08667	3834	08812	3980
08668	3835	08813	3981
08671	3838	08814	3982
08672	3839	08815	3983
08673	3840	08816	3984
08674	3841	08817	3985
08675	3842	08819	3987
08677	3844	08820	3988
08679	3846	08821	3989
08680	3847	08826	3994
08681	3848	08827	3995
08684	3851	08828	3996
08686	3853	08829	3997
08688	3855	08831	3999
08689	3856	08837	4005
08692	3859	08838	4006
08693	3860	08839	4007
08695	3862	08840	4008
08697	3864	08841	4009
08698	3865	08842	4010
08699	3866	08843	4011
08702	3869	08844	4012
08705	3872	08848	4016
08707	3874	08849	4017
08708	3875	08851	4019
08710	3877	08852	4020
08712	3879	08854	4022
08713	3880	08855	4023
08715	3882	08856	4024
08716	3883	08857	4025
	3885	08858	4026
08718	3886	08859	4027
08719	3887	08860	4028
08720	3888	08861	4029
08722	3890	08862	4030
08723	3891	08863	4031
08725	3893	08864	4032
08726	3894	08866	4034
08727	3895	08867	4035
08728	3896	08869	4037
08729	3897	08875	4043
08731	3899	08876	4044
08733	3901	08878	4046
08734	3902	08880	4048
08736	3904	08882	4096
08739	3907	08883	4097
08740	3908	08884	4098
08741	3909	08886	4116
08744	3912	08889	4119
08745	3913	08890	4120
08746	3914	08893	4123
08747	3915	08894	4124
08748	3916	08895	4125
08750	3918	08897	4127
08751	3919	08898	4128
08753	3921	08900	4130
08755	3923	08901	4131
08758	3926	08902	4132
08760	3928	08906	4136
08761	3929	08909	4139
08763	3931	08910	4140
08768	3936	08914	4144
08770	3938	08916	4146
08771	3939	08917	4147
08775	3943	08919	4149
08776	3944	08920	4150
08777	3945	08923	4153
08778	3946	08926	4156
08779	3947	08928	4158
08789	3957	08929	4159
08791	3959	08930	4160
08792	3960	08931	4161

08932	4162	
08935	4165	
08938	4168	
08940	4170	
08941	4171	
08942	4172	
08945	4175	
08946	4176	
08949	4179	
08951	4181	
08952	4182	
08953	4183	
08955	4185	
08957	4191	
08958	4192	
08991	3273	08203
08992	3329	08259

Class 09 shunter diesel-electric 0-6-0

09003	3667	
09005	3669	
09008	3719	
09011	4099	
09013	4101	
09016	97806	4104
09020	4108	
09021	4109	
09101	08833	4001
09102	08832	4000
09103	08766	3934
09104	08749	3917
09105	08835	4003
09202	08732	3900
09203	08781	3949
09205	08620	3787

Class 10 shunter diesel-electric 0-6-0

3137	13137
3138	13138
3139	13139
3140	13140
3141	13141
3142	13142
3143	13143
3144	13144
3145	13145
3146	13146
3147	13147
3148	13148
3149	13149
3150	13150
3151	13151
3439	
3440	
3441	
3442	
3443	
3444	
3445	
3446	
3447	
3448	
3449	
3450	
3451	
3453	
3473	
3474	
3475	
3476	
3477	
3478	
3479	
3480	
3481	
3482	
3483	
3484	
3485	
3486	
3487	
3488	
3490	

3491
3492
3493
3494
3495
3496
3497
3498
3499
3500
3501
3502
3612
3613
3614
3615
3616
3617
3618
3619
3620
3621
3622
3623
3624
3625
3626
3627
3628
3629
3630
3631
3632
3633
3634
3635
3636
3637
3638
3639
3640
3641
3642
3643
3644
3645
3646
3647
3648
3649
3650
3651
4049
4050
4051
4052
4053
4054
4055
4056
4057
4058
4059
4060
4061
4062
4063
4064
4065
4066
4068
4069
4070
4071
4072
4073
4074
4075
4076
4077
4078
4079
4080

4081
4082
4083
4084
4085
4086
4087
4088
4089
4090
4091
4093
4094

Class 11 shunter diesel-electric 0-6-0

12033	7120
12034	7121
12035	7122
12036	7123
12037	7124
12038	7125
12039	7126
12040	7127
12041	7128
12042	7129
12043	7130
12044	7131

12045
12046
12047
12048
12049
12050
12051
12053
12054
12055
12056
12057
12058
12059
12060
12061
12062
12063
12064
12065
12066
12067
12068
12069
12070
12071
12072
12073
12074
12075
12076
12078
12079
12080
12081
12084
12085
12086
12087
12089
12090
12091
12092
12094
12095
12096
12097
12098
12100
12101
12102
12103
12104
12105
12106
12107

12108
12109
12110
12111
12112
12113
12114
12115
12116
12117
12118
12119
12120
12121
12122
12123
12124
12125
12126
12127
12128
12129
12130
12132
12133
12134
12135
12136
12137
12138

Class 12 shunter diesel-electric 0-6-0

15211
15212
15213
15214
15215
15216
15217
15218
15219
15220
15221
15222
15223
15225
15226
15227
15228
15229
15230
15231
15232
15233
15234
15235
15236

Class 13 shunter diesel-electric 0-6-0+0-6-0

13001	4501 (4189 + 4190)
13002	4502 (4187 + 3697)
13003	4500 (4188 + 3698)

Class 14 Type 1 diesel-hydraulic 0-6-0

9501
9503
9505
9506
9507
9508
9509
9510
9511
9512
9514
9515
9517
9519
9522
9527
9528
9530
9532
9533

9534		8508
9535		8509
9536		8510
9538		8511
9540		8512
9541		8513
9542		8514
9543		8515
9544		8516
9545		8517
9546		8518
9547		8519
9548		8520
9549		8521	S18521
9550		8522
9552		8523
9554		8524
		8525

Class 15 Type 1 diesel-electric Bo-Bo

8200		8526
8201		8527
8202		8528
8203	DB968003	8529
8204		8530
8205		8531
8206		8532
8207		8533
8208		8534
8209		8535
8210		8536
8211		8537
8212		8538
8213		8539
8214		8540
8215		8541
8216		8542
8217		8543
8218		8544
8219		8545
8220		8546
8221		8547
8222		8548
8223		8549
8224		8550
8225		8551
8226		8552
8227		8553
8228		8554
8229		8555
8230		8556
8231		8557
8232		8558
8234		8559
8235		8560
8236		8561
8237	DB968002	8562
8238		8563
8239		8564
8240		8565
8241		8566
8242		8567
8243	DB968000	8568
		8569
		8570

Class 16 Type 1 diesel-electric Bo-Bo

8400	8571
8401	8572
8402	8573
8403	8574
8404	8575
8405	8576
8406	8577
8407	8578
8408	8579
8409	8580
	8581
	8582

Class 17 Type 1 diesel-electric Bo-Bo

8500	8583
8501	8584
8502	8585
8503	8586
8504	8587
8505	8588
8506	8589
8507	8590
	8591

8592
8593
8594
8595
8596
8597
8598
8599
8600
8601
8602
8603
8604
8605
8606
8607
8608
8609
8610
8611
8612
8613
8614
8615
8616

Class 20 Type 1 diesel-electric Bo-Bo

20002	8002	
20003	8003	
20004	8004	
20005	8005	
20006	8006	
20008	8008	
20009	8009	
20010	8010	
20011	8011	
20012	8012	
20013	8013	
20014	8014	
20015	8015	
20017	8017	
20018	8018	
20019	8019	
20021	8021	
20022	8022	
20023	20301	8023
20024	8024	
20025	8025	
20026	8026	
20027	8027	
20028	8028	
20029	8029	
20030	8030	
20032	8032	
20033	8033	
20034	8034	
20035	8035	CFD2001
20036	8036	
20037	8037	
20038	8038	
20039	8039	
20040	8040	
20043	8043	
20044	8044	
20045	8045	
20046	8046	
20049	8049	
20051	8051	
20052	8052	
20053	8053	
20054	8054	
20055	8055	
20058	8058	
20061	8061	
20062	8062	
20064	8064	
20065	8065	
20067	8067	
20068	8068	
20070	8070	
20071	8071	
20072	8072	
20073	8073	
20074	8074	
20076	8076	
20077	8077	
20078	8078	
20079	8079	
20080	8080	
20082	8082	
20085	8085	
20086	8086	
20089	8089	
20090	8090	
20091	8091	
20092	8092	
20093	8093	
20094	8094	
20097	8097	
20099	8099	
20100	8100	
20103	8103	
20105	8105	
20106	8106	
20108	8108	
20109	8109	
20111	8111	
20112	8112	
20113	8113	
20114	8114	
20115	8115	
20116	8116	
20119	8119	
20122	8122	
20123	8123	
20124	8124	
20125	8125	
20126	8126	
20129	8129	
20130	8130	
20133	8133	
20134	20303	8134
20135	8135	
20136	8136	
20138	8138	
20139	8139	CFD2003
20140	8140	
20141	8141	
20143	8143	
20144	8144	
20145	8145	
20146	8146	
20147	8147	
20148	8148	
20149	8149	
20150	8150	
20151	8151	
20152	8152	
20153	8153	
20155	8155	
20156	8156	
20157	8157	
20158	8158	
20159	8159	
20160	8160	
20161	8161	
20162	8162	
20163	8163	
20164	8164	
20165	8165	
20167	8167	
20170	8170	
20171	8171	
20172	20305	8172
20173	20306	8173
20174	8174	
20175	8175	
20176	8176	
20177	8177	
20178	8178	
20179	8179	
20180	8180	
20181	8181	
20182	8182	
20183	8183	
20184	8184	

20185	8185	
20186	8186	
20191	8191	
20192	8192	
20193	8193	
20195	8195	
20196	20308	8196
20197	8197	
20198	8198	
20199	8199	
20200	8300	
20201	8301	
20202	8302	
20203	8303	
20204	8304	
20206	8306	
20207	8307	
20208	8308	
20209	8309	
20210	8310	
20211	8311	
20212	8312	
20213	8313	
20215	8315	
20216	8316	
20217	8317	
20218	8318	
20220	8320	
20221	8321	
20222	8322	
20223	8323	
20224	8324	
20226	8326	
20306	20131	8131
20307	20128	8050
20310	20190	8190
20313	20194	20307	8194
20315	20104	8104
20902	20060	8060

Note: Numbers 20301-308 were used twice

Class 21 Type 2 diesel-electric Bo-Bo

6104
6105
6109
6110
6111
6115
6117
6118
6120
6122
6125
6126
6127
6128
6131
6134
6135
6136
6138
6139
6140
6141
6142
6143
6144
6145
6146
6147
6148
6149
6150
6151
6152
6153
6154
6155
6156
6157

Class 22 Type 2 diesel-hydraulic B-B
6300

6301
6302
6303
6304
6305
6306
6307
6308
6309
6310
6311
6312
6313
6314
6315
6316
6317
6318
6319
6320
6321
6322
6323
6324
6325
6326
6327
6328
6329
6330
6331
6332
6333
6334
6335
6336
6337
6338
6339
6340
6341
6342
6343
6344
6345
6346
6347
6348
6349
6350
6351
6352
6353
6354
6355
6356
6357

Class 23 Type 2 diesel-electric Bo-Bo
5900
5901
5902
5903
5904
5905
5906
5907
5908
5909

Class 24 Type 2 diesel-electric Bo-Bo

24001	5001
24002	5002
24003	5003
24004	5004
	5005
24005	5000
24006	5006
24007	5007
24008	5008
24009	5009
24010	5010
24011	5011

24012	5012		24099	5099
24013	5013		24100	5100
24014	5014		24101	5101
24015	5015		24102	5102
24016	5016		24103	5103
24017	5017		24104	5104
24018	5018		24105	5105
24019	5019		24106	5106
24020	5020		24107	5107
24021	5021		24108	5108
24022	5022		24109	5109
24023	5023		24110	5110
24024	5024		24111	5111
24025	5025		24112	5112
24026	5026		24113	5113
24027	5027			5114
	5028		24115	5115
24029	5029		24116	5116
24030	5030		24117	5117
24031	5031		24118	5118
24033	5033		24119	5119
24034	5034		24120	5120
24035	5035		24121	5121
24036	5036			5122
24037	5037		24123	5123
24038	5038		24124	5124
24039	5039		24125	5125
24040	5040		24126	5126
24041	5041		24127	5127
24042	5042		24128	5128
	5043		24129	5129
24044	5044		24130	5130
24045	5045			5131
24046	5046		24132	5132
24047	5047		24133	5133
24048	5048		24134	5134
24049	5049		24135	5135
24050	5050		24136	5136
	5051		24137	5137
24052	5052			5138
24053	5053			5139
24055	5055		24140	5140
24056	5056		24141	5141
24057	5057		24142	5142	TDB968009
24058	5058		24143	5143
24059	5059		24144	5144
24060	5060		24145	5145
24062	5062		24146	5146
24063	5063		24147	5147
24064	5064		24148	5148
24065	5065			5149
24066	5066		24150	5150
	5067			
	5068		**Class 25 Type 2 diesel-electric Bo-Bo**	
24069	5069		25001	5151
24070	5070		25002	5152
24071	5071		25003	5153
24072	5072		25004	5154
24073	5073		25005	5155
24074	5074		25006	5156
24075	5075		25007	5157
24076	5076		25008	5158
24077	5077		25009	5159
24078	5078		25010	5160
24079	5079		25011	5161
24080	5080		25012	5162
24082	5082		25013	5163
24083	5083		25014	5164
24084	5084		25015	5165
24085	5085		25016	5166
24086	5086		25017	5167
24087	5087		25018	5168
	5088		25019	5169
24089	5089		25020	5170
24090	5090		25021	5171
24091	5091		25022	5172
24092	5092		25023	5173
	5093		25024	5174
24094	5094		25025	5175
24095	5095		25026	5176
24096	5096		25027	5177
24097	5097		25028	5178
24098	5098		25029	5179

25030	5180	25119	5269	
25031	5181	25120	5270	
25032	5182	25121	5271	
25033	5183	25122	5272	
25034	5184	25123	5273	
25036	5186	25124	5274	
25037	5187	25125	5275	
25038	5188	25126	5276	
25039	5189	25127	5277	
25040	5180		5278	
25041	5191	25129	5279	
25042	5192	25130	5280	
25043	5193	25131	5281	97202
25044	5194	25132	5282	
25045	5195	25133	5283	
25046	5196	25134	5284	
25047	5197	25135	5285	
25048	5198	25136	5286	
25049	5199	25137	5287	
25050	5200	25138	5288	
25051	5201	25139	5289	
25052	5202	25140	5290	
25053	5203	25141	5291	
25054	5204	25142	5292	
25055	5205	25143	5293	
25056	5206	25144	5294	
25058	5208	25145	5295	
25060	5210	25146	5296	
25061	5211	25147	5297	
25062	5212	25148	5298	
25063	5213	25149	5299	
25064	5214	25150	7500	
25065	5215	25151	7501	
25066	5216	25152	7502	
25068	5218	25153	7503	
25069	5219	25154	7504	
25070	5220	25155	7505	
25071	5221	25156	7506	
25073	5223	25157	7507	
25074	5224	25158	7508	
25075	5225	25159	7509	
25076	5226	25160	7510	
25077	5227	25161	7511	
25078	5228	25162	7512	
25079	5229	25163	7513	
25080	5230	25164	7514	
25081	5231	25165	7515	
25082	5232	25166	7516	
25084	5234	25167	7517	
25085	5235	25168	7518	
25086	5236	25169	7519	
25087	5237	25170	7520	
25088	5238	25171	7521	
25089	5239	25172	7522	
25090	5240	25174	7524	
25091	5241	25175	7525	
25092	5242	25176	7526	
25093	5243	25177	7527	
25094	5244	25178	7528	
25095	5245	25179	7529	
25096	5246	25180	7530	
25097	5247	25181	7531	
25098	5248	25182	7532	
25099	5249	25183	7533	
25100	5250	25184	7534	
25101	5251	25186	7536	
25102	5252	25187	7537	
25103	5253	25188	7538	
25104	5254	25189	7539	
25105	5255	25190	7540	
25106	5256	25192	7542	
25107	5257	25193	7543	
25108	5258	25194	7544	
25109	5259	25195	7545	
25110	5260	25196	7546	
25111	5261	25197	7547	
25112	5262	25198	7548	
25113	5263	25199	7549	
25114	5264	25200	7550	
25115	5265	25201	7551	
25116	5266	25202	7552	
25117	5267	25203	7553	
25118	5268	25204	7554	

25205	7555	
25206	7556	
25207	7557	
25208	7558	
25209	7559	
25210	7560	
25211	7561	
25212	7562	
25213	7563	
25214	7564	
25215	7565	
25216	7566	
25217	7567	
25218	7568	
25219	7569	
25220	7570	
25221	7571	
25222	7572	
25223	7573	
25224	7574	
25225	7575	
25226	7576	
25227	7577	
25228	7578	
25229	7579	
25230	7580	
25231	7581	
25232	7582	
25233	7583	
25234	7584	
25235	7585	
25236	7586	
25237	7587	
25238	7588	
25239	7589	
25240	7590	
25241	7591	
25242	7592	
25243	7593	
25245	7595	
25246	7596	
25247	7597	
25248	7598	
25249	7599	
25250	7600	
25251	7601	
25252	7602	
25253	7603	
25254	7604	
	7605	
25256	7606	
25257	7607	
25258	7608	
25259	7609	
25260	7610	
25261	7611	
25263	7613	
25264	7614	
25266	7616	
25267	7617	
25269	7619	
25270	7620	
25271	7621	
25272	7622	
25273	7623	
25274	7624	
25275	7625	
25277	7627	
25280	7630	
25281	7631	
25282	7632	
25284	7634	
25285	7635	
25287	7637	
25288	7638	
25289	7639	
25290	7640	
25291	7641	
25292	7642	
25293	7643	
25294	7644	
25295	7645	
25298	7648	

25299	7649	
25300	7650	
25301	7651	
25302	7652	
25303	7653	
25304	7654	
25305	7655	97251
25306	7656	
25308	7658	
25310	7660	97250
25311	7661	
25312	7662	
25314	7664	97252
25317	7667	
25318	7668	
25319	7669	
25320	7670	
25321	7671	
25323	7673	
25324	7674	
25325	7675	
25326	7676	
25327	7677	
25902	25268	7618
25903	25276	7626
25905	25286	7636
25906	25296	7646
25907	25297	7647
25908	25307	7657
25910	25315	7665
25911	25316	7666

Class 26 Type 2 diesel-electric Bo-Bo

26003	5303
26005	5305
26006	5306
26008	5308
26009	5309
26012	5312
26013	5313
26015	5315
26016	5316
26017	5317
26018	5318
26019	5319
26020	5307
26021	5321
26022	5322
26023	5323
26026	5326
26027	5327
	5328
26028	5320
26029	5329
26030	5330
26031	5331
26032	5332
26033	5333
26034	5334
26036	5336
26037	5337
26039	5339
26041	5341
26042	5342
26044	5344
26045	5345
26046	5346

Class 27 Type 2 diesel-electric Bo-Bo

27002	5348
27003	5349
27004	5350
27006	5352
27008	5354
27009	5355
27010	5356
27011	5357
27012	5358
27013	5359
27014	5360
27015	5361
27016	5362
27017	5363

27018	5364		
27019	5365		
27020	5366		
27021	5367		
27022	5368		
27023	5369		
27025	5371		
27026	5372		
27027	5373		
27028	5375		
27029	5376		
27030	5377		
27031	5378		
27032	5379		
27033	5381		
27034	5382		
	5383		
27035	5384		
27036	5385		
27037	5389		
27038	5390		
27039	5398		
27040	5402		
27041	5405		
27042	5406		
27043	5414		
27044	5415		
27045	27101	5374	
27046	27102	5380	
27047	27103	27118	5413
27048	27104	5387	
27049	27105	5388	
27051	27107	5395	
27052	27108	5396	
27053	27109	5397	
27054	27110	5399	
27055	27111	5400	
27058	27204	27122	5403
27063	27209	27115	5408
27064	27210	27116	5409
27065	27211	27117	5411
27201	27119	5391	
27202	27120	5392	
27203	27121	5393	
27206	27124	5412	
27207	ADB968025		
	27113	5404	
27208	27114	5407	

Note: Number 27103 was used twice

Class 28 Type 2 diesel-electric Co-Bo

5700
5701
5702
5703
5704
5706
5707
5708
5709
5710
5711
5712
5713
5714
5715
5716
5717
5718
5719

Class 29 Type 2 diesel-electric Bo-Bo

6100
6101
6102
6103
6106
6107
6108
6112
6113
6114
6116
6119
6121
6123
6124
6129
6130
6132
6133
6137

Class 31 Type 2 diesel-electric A1A-A1A

31001	5501	
31002	5502	ADB968014
31003	5503	
31004	5504	
31005	5505	
31006	5506	
31007	5507	
31008	5508	ADB968016
31009	5509	
31010	5510	
31011	5511	
31012	5512	
31013	5513	
31014	5514	ADB968015
31015	5515	
31016	5516	
31017	5517	
31019	5519	
31102	5520	
31103	5521	
31107	5525	
31109	5527	
31110	5528	
31111	5529	
31112	5530	
31113	5531	
31116	5534	
31117	5535	
31118	5536	
31120	5538	
31121	5539	
31122	5540	
31123	5541	
31124	5542	
31125	5543	
31126	5544	
31127	5545	
31131	5549	
31132	5550	
31134	5552	
31135	5553	
31136	5554	
31138	5556	
31141	5559	
31142	5560	
31143	5561	
31144	5562	
31145	5563	
31146	5564	
31147	5565	
31149	5567	
31150	5568	
31152	5570	
31154	5572	
31155	5573	
31156	5574	
31158	5576	
31159	5577	
31160	5578	
31164	5582	
31165	5583	
31166	5584	
31167	5585	
31168	5586	
31170	5588	
31171	5590	
31173	5593	
31174	5594	
31175	5595	
31176	5597	
31178	5599	
31180	5601	

31181	5602
31183	5604
31184	5607
31185	5608
31187	5610
31188	5611
31189	5612
31192	5615
31195	5619
31196	5620
31198	5622
31199	5623
31200	5624
31201	5625
31202	5626
31205	5629
31208	5632
31209	5633
31212	5636
31214	5638
31215	5639
31217	5642
31218	5643
31219	5644
31221	5647
31222	5648
31223	5649
31224	5650
31225	5651
31226	5652
31227	5653
31229	5655
31230	5657
31231	5658
31232	5659
31234	5661
31237	5664
31238	5665
31240	5667
31241	5668
31242	5670
31243	5671
31244	5672
31245	5673
31247	5675
31248	5676
31249	5677
31250	5678
31252	5680
31254	5682
31257	5685
31259	5687
31260	5688
31261	5689
31262	5690
31263	5693
31264	5694
31268	5698
31272	5802
31273	5803
31275	5805
31276	5806
31278	5808
31280	5810
31281	5811
31282	5813
31283	5815
31284	5816
31286	5818
31287	5819
31288	5820
31290	5822
31292	5825
31293	5826
31294	5827
31296	5829
31298	5831	97203
31299	5832
31301	5834
31302	5835
31304	5837
31305	5838
31306	5839

31308	5841		
31309	5843		
31311	5845		
31312	5846		
31313	5847		
31314	5848		
31317	5851		
31319	5853		
31320	5854		
31322	5857		
31323	5858		
31324	5859		
31400	31161	5579	
31401	5589		
31402	5592		
31403	5596		
31404	5605		
31405	5606		
31406	5616		
31407	31507	5640	
31408	5646		
31409	5656		
31410	5669		
31411	31511	5691	
31412	31512	5692	
31413	5812		
31415	5824		
31417	5856		
31420	31172	5591	
31421	31140	5558	
31422	31522	31310	5844
31423	31197	5621	
31425	31274	5804	
31426	31526	31193	5617
31427	31194	5618	
31428	31211	5635	
31429	31269	5699	
31432	31153	5571	
31433	31533	31236	5663
31434	31258	5686	
31436	31151	5569	
31437	31537	31182	5603
31439	31239	5666	
31440	31204	5628	
31442	31251	5679	
31443	31177	5598	
31444	31544	31137	5555
31450	31133	5551	
31455	31555	31246	5674
31457	31169	5587	
31460	31266	5696	
31462	31315	5849	
31464	31325	5860	
31467	31216	5641	
31468	31568	31321	5855
31516	31416	5842	
31519	31419	5697	
31524	31424	31157	5575
31531	31431	31253	5681
31541	31441	31220	5645
31545	31445	31300	5833
31546	31446	31316	5850
31547	31447	31295	5828
31548	31448	31148	5566
31549	31449	31307	5840
31551	31451	31318	5852
31553	31453	31114	5532
31556	31456	31291	5823
31558	31458	31303	5836
31569	31469	31277	5807
31602	31191	5614	
31970	97204	31326	5861

Class 33 Type 3 diesel-electric Bo-Bo

33001	6500
	6502
33003	6503
33004	6504
33005	6505
33006	6506
33007	6507
33009	6509
33010	6510

33011	6512	
33013	6518	
33014	6522	
33015	6523	
33016	6524	
33017	6526	
33020	6537	
33022	6540	
33023	6541	
33024	6542	
33026	6544	
33027	6545	
33028	6546	
33031	6549	
33032	6550	
33033	6551	
33034	6552	
33036	6554	
33037	6555	
33038	6556	
33039	6557	
33040	6558	
33041	6559	
33042	6560	
33043	6561	
33044	6562	
33045	6563	
33047	6565	
33049	6567	
33050	6568	
33051	6569	
33054	6572	
33055	6573	
33056	6574	
	6576	
33058	6577	
33059	6578	
33060	6579	
33061	6581	
33062	6582	
33064	6584	
33101	6511	
33104	6516	
33105	6517	
33106	6519	
33107	6520	
33112	6529	
33113	6531	
33114	6532	
33115	83301	6533
33118	6538	
33119	6580	
33203	6588	
33204	6589	
33205	33302	6590
33206	6591	
33209	6594	
33210	6595	
33211	6596	
33212	6597	

Class 35 Type 3 diesel-hydraulic B-B

7000	
7001	
7002	
7003	
7004	
7005	
7006	
7007	
7008	
7009	
7010	
7011	
7012	
7013	
7014	
7015	
7016	
7019	
7020	
7021	
7022	
7023	
7024	
7025	
7026	
7027	
7028	
7030	
7031	
7032	
7033	
7034	
7035	
7036	
7037	
7038	
7039	
7040	
7041	
7042	
7043	
7044	
7045	
7046	
7047	
7048	
7049	
7050	
7051	
7052	
7053	
7054	
7055	DB968004
7056	
7057	
7058	
7059	
7060	
7061	
7062	
7063	
7064	
7065	
7066	
7067	
7068	
7069	
7070	
7071	
7072	
7073	
7074	
7075	
7077	
7078	
7079	
7080	
7081	
7082	
7083	
7084	
7085	
7086	
7087	
7088	
7089	TDB968005
7090	
7091	
7092	
7093	
7094	
7095	
7096	
7097	
7098	
7099	
7100	

Class 37 Type 3 diesel-electric Co-Co

37004	6704	
37008	37352	6708
37010	6710	
37011	6711	
37012	6712	

37013	6713	
37019	6719	
37026	37320	6726
37031	6731	
37035	6735	
37040	6740	
37043	37354	6743
37045	37355	6745
37046	6746	
37047	6747	
37048	6748	
37051	6751	
37054	6754	
37055	6755	
37058	6758	
37062	6762	
37063	6763	
37065	6765	
37066	6766	
37068	37356	6768
37070	6770	
37071	6771	
37072	6772	
37073	6773	
37074	6774	
37077	6777	
37078	6778	
37079	37357	6779
37080	6780	
37083	6783	
37087	6787	
37088	37323	6788
37092	6792	
37095	6795	
37096	6796	
37098	6798	
37104	6804	
37106	6806	
37107	6807	
37110	6810	
37111	37326	6811
37113	6813	
37114	6814	
37131	6831	
37133	6833	
37137	37312	6837
37138	6838	
37139	6839	
37140	6840	
37141	6841	
37144	6844	
37153	6853	
37154	6854	
37156	37311	6856
37158	6858	
37162	6862	
37174	6874	
37184	6884	
37185	6885	
37188	6888	
37191	6891	
37194	6894	
37196	6896	
37197	6897	
37201	6901	
37203	6903	
37209	6909	
37211	6911	
37212	6912	
37213	6913	
37220	6920	
37221	6921	
37222	6922	
37223	6923	
37225	6925	
37229	6929	
37230	6930	
37232	6932	
37235	6935	
37238	6938	
37241	6941	
37242	6942	
37244	6944	

37245	6945		
37251	6951		
37252	6952		
37260	6960		
37262	6962		
37273	37306	6606	
37278	6978		
37280	6980		
	6983		
37293	6993		
37298	6998		
37330	37128	6828	
37331	37202	6902	
37332	37239	6939	
37333	37271	37303	6603
37334	37272	37304	6604
37335	37285	6985	
37341	37015	6715	
37343	37049	37322	6749
37344	37053	6753	
37345	37101	6801	
37351	37002	6702	
37358	37091	6791	
37359	37118	6818	
37370	37127	6827	
37371	37147	6847	
37372	37159	6859*	
37373	37160	6860	
37375	37193	6893	
37376	37199	6899	
37377	37200	6900	
37378	37204	6904	
37379	37226	6926	
37381	37284	6984	
37382	37145	37313	6845
37383	37167	6867	
37384	37258	6958	
37404	37286	6986	
37406	37295	6995	
37408	37289	6989	
37410	37273	6973	
37411	37290	6990	
37412	37301	6601	
37413	37276	6976	
37414	37287	6987	
37415	37277	6977	
37416	37302	6602	
37417	37269	6969	
37420	37297	6997	
37426	37299	6999	
37427	37288	6988	
37428	37281	6981	
37429	37300	6600	
37430	37265	6965	
37431	37272	6972	
37505	37028	6728	
37509	37093	6793	
37513	37056	6756	
37515	37064	6764	
37519	37027	6727	
37520	37041	6741	
37670	37182	6882	
37671	37247	6947	
37672	37189	6889	
37673	37132	6832	
37675	37164	6864	
37677	37121	6821	
37678	37256	6956	
37680	37224	6924	
37681	37130	6830	
37682	37236	6936	
37683	37187	6877	
37684	37134	6834	
37686	37172	6872	
37689	37195	6895	
37692	37122	6822	
37693	37210	6910	
37694	37192	6892	
37695	37157	6857	
37696	37228	6928	
37697	37243	6943	
37698	37246	6946	
37699	37253	6953	

37701	37030	6730
37702	37020	6720
37704	37034	6734
37705	37060	6760
37707	37001	6701
37708	37089	6789
37709	37014	6714
37711	37085	6785
37713	37052	6752
37715	37021	6721
37717	37050	6750
37718	37084	6784
37719	37033	6733
37796	37105	6805
37797	37081	6781
37798	37006	6706
37799	37061	6761
37801	37173	6873
37802	37163	6863
37803	37208	6908
37883	37176	6876
37885	37177	6877
37886	37180	6880
37887	37120	6820
37888	37135	6835
37889	37233	6933
37890	37168	6868
37891	37166	6866
37892	37149	6849
37893	37237	6937
37894	37124	6824
37895	37283	6819
37896	37231	6931
37897	37155	6855
37898	37186	6886
37899	37161	6861
37902	37148	6848
37903	37249	6949
37904	37125	6825

Note: Numbers 37271-274 were used twice
*37372 donated parts of its body to the construction of D5910

Class 40 Type 4 diesel-electric 1Co-Co1

40001	201	40041	241	
40002	202	40042	242	
40003	203	40043	243	
40004	204	40044	244	
40005	205	40045	245	
40006	206	40046	246	
40007	207	40047	247	
40008	208	40048	248	
40009	209	40049	249	
40010	210	40050	250	
40011	211	40051	251	
40014	214	40052	252	
40015	215	40053	253	
40016	216	40054	254	
40017	217	40055	255	
40018	218	40056	256	
40019	219	40057	257	
40020	220	40058	258	
40021	221	40059	259	
40022	222	40060	260	97405
40023	223	40061	261	
40024	224	40062	262	
40025	225	40063	263	
40026	226	40064	264	
40027	227	40065	265	
40028	228	40066	266	
40029	229	40067	267	
40030	230	40068	268	
40031	231	40069	269	
40032	232	40070	270	
40033	233	40071	271	
40034	234	40072	272	
40035	235	40073	273	
40036	236	40074	274	
40037	237	40075	275	
40038	238	40076	276	
40039	239	40077	277	
40040	240	40078	278	
		40079	279	
		40080	280	
		40081	281	
		40082	282	
		40083	283	
		40084	284	
		40085	285	
		40086	286	
		40087	287	
		40088	288	
		40089	289	
		40090	290	
		40091	291	
		40092	292	
		40093	293	
		40094	294	
		40095	295	
		40096	296	
		40097	297	
		40098	298	
		40099	299	
		40100	300	
		40101	301	
		40102	302	
		40103	303	
		40104	304	
		40105	305	
		40107	307	
		40108	308	
		40109	309	
		40110	310	
		40111	311	
		40112	312	
		40113	313	
		40114	314	
		40115	315	
		40116	316	
		40117	317	
		40119	319	
		40120	320	
		40121	321	
			322	
		40123	323	
		40124	324	
		40125	325	

40126	326
40127	327
40128	328
40129	329
40130	330
40131	331
40132	332
40133	333
40134	334
40136	336
40137	337
40138	338
40139	339
40140	340
40141	341
40142	342
40143	343
40144	344
40146	346
40147	347
40148	348
40149	349
40150	350
40151	351
40152	352
40153	353
40154	354
40155	355
40156	356
40157	357
40158	358
40159	359
40160	360
40161	361
40162	362
40163	363
40164	364
40165	365
40166	366
40167	367
40168	368
40169	369
40170	370
40171	371
40172	372
40173	373
40174	374
40175	375
40176	376
40177	377
40178	378
40179	379
40180	380
40181	381
40182	382
40183	383
40184	384
40185	385
40186	386
40187	387
40188	388
40189	389
40190	390
40191	391
40192	392
40193	393
40194	394
40195	395
40196	396
40197	397
40198	398
40199	399

Class 41 Type 4 diesel-hydraulic A1A-A1A
600
601
602
603
604

Class 42 Type 4 diesel-hydraulic B-B
800
801

802
803
804
805
806
807
808
809
810
811
812
813
814
815
816
817
818
819
820
822
823
824
825
826
827
828
829
830
831
866
867
868
869
870

Class 43 Type 4 diesel-hydraulic B-B
833
834
835
836
837
838
839
840
841
842
843
844
845
846
847
848
849
850
851
852
853
854
855
856
857
858
859
860
861
862
863
864
865

Class 41/43 Type 4 diesel-electric Bo-Bo (HST power car)

41002	43001	ADB975813

Class 43 Type 4 diesel-electric Bo-Bo (HST power car)
43011
43019
43173

Class 44 Type 4 diesel-electric 1Co-Co1

44001	1
44002	2
44003	3

44005	5
44006	6
44007	7
44009	9
44010	10

Class 45 Type 4 diesel-electric 1Co-Co1

45001	13	
45002	29	
45003	133	
45004	77	
45005	79	
45006	89	
45007	119	
45008	90	
45009	37	
45010	112	
45011	12	
45012	108	
45013	20	
45014	137	
45016	16	
45017	23	ADB968024
45018	15	
45019	33	
45020	26	
45021	25	
45022	60	97409
45023	54	
45024	17	
45025	19	
45026	21	
45027	24	
45028	27	
45029	30	97410
45030	31	
45031	36	
45032	38	
45033	39	
45034	42	97411
45035	44	
45036	45	
45037	46	
45038	48	
45039	49	
45040	50	97412
45042	57	
45043	58	
45044	63	
45045	64	
45046	68	
45047	69	
45048	70	
45049	71	
45050	72	
45051	74	
45052	75	
45053	76	
45054	95	
45055	84	
45056	91	
45057	93	
45058	97	
45059	98	
45061	101	
45062	103	
45063	104	
45064	105	
45065	110	
45066	114	97413
45067	115	
45068	118	
45069	121	
45070	122	
45071	125	
45072	127	
45073	129	
45074	131	
45075	132	
45076	134	
45077	136	
45101	96	
45102	51	

45103	116	
45104	59	
45106	106	
45107	43	
45109	85	
45110	73	
45111	65	
45113	80	
45114	94	
45115	81	
45116	47	
45117	35	
45119	34	
45120	107	
45121	18	
45122	11	
45123	52	
45124	28	
45126	32	
45127	87	
45128	113	
45129	111	
45130	117	
45131	124	
45134	126	
45136	88	
45137	56	
45138	92	
45139	109	
45140	102	
45141	82	
45142	83	
45143	62	
45144	55	
45145	128	
45146	66	
45147	41	
45148	130	
45150	45054	78

Note: Number 45054 was used twice

Class 46 Type 4 diesel-electric 1Co-Co1

46001	138
46002	139
46003	140
46004	141
46005	142
46006	143
46007	144
46008	145
46009	146
46011	148
46012	149
46013	150
46014	151
46015	152
46016	153
46017	154
46018	155
46019	156
46020	157
46021	158
46022	159
46023	160
46024	161
46025	162
46026	163
46027	164
46028	165
46029	166
46030	167
46031	168
46032	169
46033	170
46034	171
46036	173
46037	174
46038	175
46039	176
46040	177
46041	178
46042	179
46043	180

46044	181
46046	183
46047	184
46048	185
46049	186
46050	187
46051	188
46052	189
46053	190
46054	191
46055	192
46056	193

Class 47 Type 4 diesel-electric Co-Co

47001	1521
47002	1522
47003	1523
47005	1526
47006	1528
47007	1529
47008	1530
47009	1532
47010	1537
47011	1538
47012	1539
47013	1540
47014	1543
47015	1544
47016	1546
47017	1570
47018	1572
47019	1573
47033	1613
47049	1631
47050	1632
47051	1633
47052	1634
47053	1635
47054	1638
47063	1647
47085	1670
	1671
47089	1675
47093	1679
47094	1680
47095	1681
47096	1682
47097	1684
47098	1685
47099	1686
47100	1687
47101	1688
47102	1690
47103	1691
47104	1692
47106	1694
47107	1695
47108	1696
47109	1697
47110	1698
47111	1699
47112	1700
47113	1701
47114	1702
47115	1703
47116	1704
47118	1706
47119	1708
47120	1709
47121	1710
47122	1711
47123	1712
47124	1714
47125	1715
47130	1721
47131	1722
47137	1729
47140	1732
	1734
47142	1735
47143	1736
47144	1737
47145	1738

47146	1739	
47147	1740	
47148	1741	
47150	47399	1743
47152	47398	1745
47156	1749	
47157	1750	
47159	1752	
47162	1756	
47186	1781	
47188	1838	
47189	1839	
47190	1840	
47191	1841	
47193	1843	
47195	1845	
47196	1846	
47197	1847	
47198	1848	
47199	1849	
47200	1850	
47201	1851	
47202	1852	
47203	1853	
47207	1857	
47208	1858	
47210	1860	
47211	47394	1861
47212	1862	
47213	1863	
47214	1864	
47215	1865	
47217	1867	
47218	1868	
47219	1869	
47220	1870	
47221	1871	
47222	1872	
47223	1873	
47224	1874	
47226	47384	1902
47227	1903	
47228	1904	
47229	1905	
47230	1906	
	1908	
47233	1910	
47235	1912	
47236	1913	
47238	1915	
47241	1918	
47249	1926	
47256	1934	
47258	1938	
47275	1977	
47276	1978	
47277	1979	
47278	1980	
47279	1981	
47280	1982	
47281	1983	
47282	1984	
47283	1985	
47284	1986	
47285	1987	
47286	1988	
47287	1989	
47288	1990	
47289	1991	
47291	1993	
47293	1995	
47294	1996	
47295	1997	
47296	1998	
47297	1999	
47298	1100	
47299	47216	1866
47300	47468	1594
47301	1782	
47302	1783	
47303	47397	1784
47304	47392	1785
47305	1786	

47307	1788		47430	1542	
47308	1789		47431	1545	
47309	47389	1790	47432	1547	
47310	1791		47433	1548	
47311	1792		47434	1549	
47312	1793		47435	1550	
47313	1794		47436	1552	
47314	47387	1795	47437	1553	
47315	1796		47438	1554	
47316	1797		47439	1555	
47318	1799		47440	1556	
47319	1800		47441	1557	
47320	1801		47442	1558	
47321	1802		47443	1559	
47323	1804		47444	1560	
47324	1805		47445	1561	
47325	1806			1562	
47326	1807		47446	1563	
47327	1808		47447	1564	
47328	47396	1809	47448	1565	
47331	1812		47450	1567	
47333	1814		47451	1568	
47334	1815		47452	1569	
47335	1816		47453	1571	
47336	1817		47454	1574	
47338	1819		47455	1575	
47339	1820		47456	1576	
47340	1821		47457	1577	
47341	1822		47458	1578	
47342	1823		47459	1579	
47343	1824		47460	1580	
47344	1825		47461	1581	
47345	1826		47462	1582	
47346	1827		47463	1586	
47348	1829		47464	1587	
47351	1832		47465	1589	
47352	1833		47466	1590	
47353	1834		47467	1593	
47354	1835		47469	1595	
47357	1876		47470	1596	
47358	1877		47471	1598	
47359	1878		47472	97472	1600
47360	1879		47473	1601	
47361	1880		47474	1602	
47362	1881		47475	1603	
47363	47385	1882	47476	1604	
47365	1884		47477	1607	
47366	1885		47478	1608	
47369	1888		47479	1612	
47370	1889		47481	1627	
47373	1892		47482	1636	
47374	1893		47483	1637	
47377	1896		47485	1683	
47378	47386	1897	47486	1689	
47379	1898		47487	1707	
47380	1899		47489	1716	
47381	1900		47500	47770	1943
47403	1502		47508	1952	
47404	1503		47509	1953	
47405	1504		47512	1958	
47406	1505		47513	1959	
47407	1506		47515	1961	
47408	1507		47518	1101	
47409	1508		47519	1102	
47410	1509		47520	1103	
47411	1510		47521	1104	
47412	1511		47522	1105	
47413	1512		47523	1106	
47414	1513		47524	1107	
47415	1514		47525	1108	
47416	1515		47527	1110	
47418	1517		47528	1111	
47419	1518		47529	1551	
47420	1519		47530	1930	
47421	1520		47532	1641	
47422	1525		47533	1651	
47423	1527		47534	1678	
47424	1531		47535	1649	
47425	1533		47536	1655	
47426	1534		47538	1669	ADB968035
47427	1535		47539	1718	
47428	1536		47540	47975	1723
47429	1541		47542	1585	

47543	1588			
47544	1592			
47547	1642			
47549	47133	1724		
47550	1731			
47555	47126	1717		
47565	47039	1620		
47566	47043	1624		
47572	47168	1763		
47574	47174	1769		
47575	47175	1770		
47576	47176	1771		
47584	47180	1775		
47624	47087	1673		
47627	47273	1974		
47628	47078	1663		
47633	47083	1668		
47634	47158	1751		
47645	47075	1659		
47676	47586	47042	1623	
47677	47617	47149	1742	
47702	47504	1947		
47704	47495	1937		
47706	47494	1936		
47707	47506	1949		
47708	47516	1968		
47709	47499	1942		
47710	47496	1939		
47711	47498	1941		
47713	47510	1954		
47716	47507	1957		
47717	47497	1940		
47721	47557	47024	1591	
47722	47558	47027	1599	
47725	47567	47044	1625	
47726	47568	47045	1626	
47733	47582	47170	1765	
47734	47583	47172	1767	
47736	47587	47263	1963	
47737	47588	47178	1773	
47738	47592	47171	1766	
47741	47597	47026	1597	
47742	47598	47182	1777	
47743	47599	47177	1772	
47745	47603	47267	1967	
47747	47615	47252	1929	
47750	47626	47082	1667	
47756	47644	47246	1923	
47757	47585	47184	1779	
47758	47517	1975		
47759	47559	47028	1605	
47762	47573	47173	1768	
47763	47581	47169	1764	
47764	47630	47041	1622	
47766	47642	47040	1621	
47767	47641	47086	1672	
47774	47801	47551	47153	1746
47775	47531	47974	1584	
47777	47243	47636	1920	
47778	47842	47606	47081	1666
47779	47838	47612	47080	1665
47780	47836	47618	47030	1609
47781	47808	47653	47088	1674
47782	47824	47602	47185	1780
47783	47809	47654	47056	1640
47784	47819	47664	47135	1727
47788	47833	47608	47262	1962
47789	47671	47616	47248	1925
47791	47675	47595	47268	1969
47803	47553	47260	1956	
47829	47619	47264	1964	
47837	47611	47166	1761	
47839	47621	47136	1728	
47844	47556	47020	1583	
47849	47570	47048	1744	
47850	47648	47151	1744	
47852	47646	47074	1658	
47901	47601	47046	1628	
47971	97480	47480	1616	
47972	97545	47545	1646	
47973	97561	47561	47034	1614
47976	47546	1747		
47981	47364	1883		

Class 50 Type 4 diesel-electric Co-Co

50001	401
50003	403
50004	404
50005	405
50006	406
50009	409
50010	410
50011	411
50012	412
50013	413
50014	414
50016	416
50018	418
50020	420
50022	422
50023	423
50024	424
50025	425
50028	428
50032	432
50034	434
50036	436
50037	437
50038	438
50039	439
50040	440
50041	441
50043	443
50045	445
50046	446
50047	447
50048	448

Class 52 Type 4 diesel-hydraulic C-C

1000
1001
1002
1003
1004
1005
1006
1007
1008
1009
1011
1012
1014
1016
1017
1018
1019
1020
1021
1022
1024
1025
1026
1027
1028
1029
1030
1031
1032
1033
1034
1035
1036
1037
1038
1039
1040
1042
1043
1044
1045
1046
1047
1049
1050
1051
1052
1053

1054
1055
1056
1057
1058
1059
1060
1061
1063
1064
1065
1066
1067
1068
1069
1070
1071
1072
1073

Class 53 Type 4 diesel-electric Co-Co

1200	0280

Class 55 Type 5 diesel-electric Co-Co

55001	9001
55003	9003
55004	9004
55005	9005
55006	9006
55007	9007
55008	9008
55010	9010
55011	9011
55012	9012
55013	9013
55014	9014
55017	9017
55018	9018
55020	9020
55021	9021

Class 56 Type 5 diesel-electric Co-Co

56001
56002
56004
56005
56008
56010
56011
56012
56013
56014
56015
56016
56017
56019
56020
56021
56022
56023
56024
56025
56026
56027
56028
56029
56030
56033
56034
56035
56036
56039
56040
56041
56042
56043
56044
56046
56047
56048
56050
56052
56053
56054
56055
56056
56058
56059
56061
56062
56063
56064
56066
56067
56068
56070
56071
56072
56073
56074
56075
56076
56079
56080
56082
56083
56084
56085
56086
56088
56089
56092
56093
56095
56099
56100
56102
56107
56108
56109
56110
56111
56112
56114
56116
56118
56119
56120
56121
56122
56123
56126
56127
56128
56129
56130
56131
56132
56133
56134
56135

Class 58 Type 5 diesel-electric Co-Co

58002
58003
58008
58014
58017
58019
58028
58037
58045

Class 66 Type 5 diesel-electric Co-Co

66521	
66734	66402

Class 70 Type 5 diesel-electric Co-Co

70012

Class 70 750V DC electric Co-Co

20001	CC1
20002	CC2
20003	

Class 71 750V DC electric Bo-Bo

71002	E5002	
71003	E5018	E5003
71004	E5004	

71005	E5020	E5005
71006	E5022	E5006
71007	E5007	
71008	E5008	
71009	E5009	
71010	E5010	
71011	E5011	
71012	E5012	
71013	E5013	
71014	E5014	

Note: Numbers E5003/05/06 were used twice

Class 73 750V DC Electro-diesel Bo-Bo

73004	E6004	
73106	E6012	
73108	E6014	
73111	E6017	
73115	E6021	
	E6027	
73126	E6033	
73131	E6038	
73132	E6039	
73203	73127	E6024

Class 74 750V DC Electro-diesel Bo-Bo

74001	E6101	E5015	
74002	E6102	E5016	
74003	E6103	E5006	
74004	E6104	E5000	E5024
74005	E6105	E5019	
74006	E6106	E5023	
74007	E6107	E5003	
74008	E6108	E5005	
74009	E6109	E5017	
74010	E6110	E5021	

Class 76 1,500V DC electric Bo+Bo

	E26000	6700
76001	E26001	
76002	E26002	
76003	76036	E26036
76004	E26004	
	E26005	
76006	E26006	
76007	E26007	
76008	E26008	
76009	E26009	
76010	E26010	
76011	E26011	
76012	E26012	
76013	E26013	
76014	E26014	
76015	E26015	
76016	E26016	
	E26017	
	E26019	
76021	E26021	
76022	E26022	
76023	E26023	
76024	E26024	
76025	E26025	
76026	E26026	
76027	E26027	
76028	E26028	
76029	E26029	
76030	E26030	
	E26031	
76031	76044	E26044
76032	E26032	
76033	E26033	
76034	E26034	
	E26035	
76035	76018	E26018
76036	76003	E26003
76037	E26037	
76038	76050	E26050
76039	76048	E26048
76040	E26040	
76041	E26041	
	E26042	
76043	E26043	
	E26045	
76046	E26046	

76047	E26047	
76048	76039	E26039
76049	E26049	
76050	76038	E26038
76051	E26051	
76052	E26052	
76053	E26053	
76054	E26054	
76055	E26055	
76056	E26056	
76057	E26057	

Note: Numbers 76003/036/038/039/048/050 were used twice

Class 77 1,500V DC electric Co-Co

	E27005
1503	E27004
1504	E27006
1506	E27002

Class 81 25kV AC electric Bo-Bo

81001	E3001
	E3002
81003	E3004
81004	E3005
81005	E3006
81006	E3007
81007	E3008
	E3009
81008	E3010
81009	E3011
81010	E3012
81011	E3013
81012	E3014
81013	E3015
81014	E3016
81015	E3017
81016	E3018
	E3019
81017	E3020
81018	E3021
81019	E3022
81020	E3023
81021	E3096
81022	E3097

Class 82 25kV AC electric Bo-Bo

	E3046
82001	E3047
82002	E3048
82003	E3049
82004	E3050
82005	E3051
82006	E3052
82007	E3053
	E3055

Class 83 25kV AC electric Bo-Bo

83001	E3024	
83002	E3025	
83003	E3026	
83004	E3027	
83005	E3028	
83006	E3029	
83007	E3030	
83008	E3031	
83009	E3032	
83010	E3033	
83011	E3034	
83013	E3098	E3303
83014	E3099	E3304
83015	E3100	

Class 84 25kV AC electric Bo-Bo

84002	E3037	
84003	E3038	
84004	E3039	
84005	E3040	
84006	E3041	
84007	E3042	
84008	E3043	
84009	E3044	ADB968021
84010	E3045	

Class 85 25kV AC electric Bo-Bo

85001	E3056
85002	E3057
85005	E3060
85008	E3063
85013	E3068
85014	E3069
85015	E3070
85017	E3072
85018	E3073
85019	E3074
85020	E3075
85022	E3077
85023	E3078
85025	E3080
85026	E3081
85027	E3082
85028	E3083
85029	E3084
85030	E3085
85031	E3086
85033	E3088
85034	E3089
85037	E3092
85038	E3093
85039	E3094
85040	E3095

85102	85009	E3064
85103	85010	E3065
85104	85012	E3067
85105	85016	E3071
85106	85021	E3076
85107	85024	E3079
85108	85032	E3087
85109	85035	E3090
85110	85036	E3091
85111	85004	E3059
85112	85007	E3062
85113	85003	E3058
85114	85011	E3066

Class 86 25kV AC electric Bo-Bo

86102	86202	E3150	
86103	86203	E3143	
86204	E3173		
86206	E3184		
86207	E3179		
86208	E3141		
86209	E3125		
86211	E3147		
86212	E3151		
86214	E3106		
86216	E3166		
86219	E3196		
86220	E3156		
86221	E3132		
86222	86502	E3131	
86223	E3158		
86224	E3134		
86225	E3164		
86226	E3162		
86227	E3117		
86230	E3168		
86236	E3133		
86237	E3197		
86238	E3116		
86239	86507	E3169	
86240	E3127		
86241	86508	E3121	
86243	E3181		
86244	E3178		
86245	E3182		
86246	86505	E3149	
86247	E3192		
86249	E3161		
86252	E3101		
86254	86047	E3142	
86255	86042	E3154	
86256	86040	E3135	
86257	86043	E3139	
86258	86501	86046	E3140
86261	86041	E3118	
86416	86316	86016	E3109

86417	86317	86017	E3146
86419	86319	86019	E3120
86425	86325	86025	E3186
86426	86326	86026	E3195
86429	86329	86029	E3200
86430	86030	E3105	
86602	86402	86002	E3170
86603	86403	86003	E3115
86606	86406	86006	E3112
86611	86411	86311	86011	E3171
86615	86415	86315	86015	E3123
86618	86418	86318	86018	E3163
86620	86420	86320	86020	E3114
86621	86421	86321	86021	E3157
86623	86423	86323	86023	E3152
86631	86431	86031	E3188
86633	86433	86033	E3198
86634	86434	86034	E3187
86635	86435	86035	E3124
86636	86436	86036	E3160

86901	86253	86044	E3136
86902	86210	E3190	

Note: Number 86501 was used twice by 86258 and 86608 (the latter still in traffic)

Class 87 25kV AC electric Bo-Bo

87005
87011
87015
87016
87018
87021
87024
87027
87030
87031
87032
87101

Various departmental locos

97020	20
97652	PWM652
97653	PWM653
97701	M61136
97702	M61139
97703	M61182
97704	M61185
97705	M61184
97706	M61189
97707	M61166
97708	M61173
97709	M61172
97710	M61175
ED1	
ED2	
ED3	
ED4	
ED5	
ED6	
ED7	
ED10	
ZM9	

Livery codes

ADZ   Advenza Freight blue
AGA   Abellio Greater Anglia white
AGI   Aggregates industries turquoise and silver
ANG   Anglia Railways turquoise
ATW   Arriva Trains Wales turquoise, unbranded
AVD   AV Dawson red
BAF   Bardon Aggregates blue with Freightliner branding
BBM   Battle of Britain Memorial Flight graphics
BEA   Beacon Rail Blue (GBRf)
BDB   Boston Docks blue
BIF   Biffa red bodyside, orange cabs (GBRf)
BLE   Unspecified plain blue
BLK   British Railways black
BLL   British Rail 'large logo' blue with yellow cabs
BLU   British Rail blue yellow cabsides
BMT   Bulmarket red
BRB   British Rail blue with full yellow ends
BRE   British Rail Blue with large numbers and emblems
BRF   British Rail blue with Union flags
BRL   British Rail blue large logo blue with black roof
BRP   British Rail blue grey prototype HST
BRW   British Rail blue with wasp stripes
BRY   British Railways blue with Foster Yeoman branding
BRZ   BZK BR blue
BYP   British Rail blue with small yellow panels
BZK   BZK (Българска Жеиезолътна Компания) green and yellow
CAL   Caledonian Sleeper blue
CAS   Castle Cement light grey
CCE   Civil engineers' grey/yellow 'Dutch'
CCT   Civil engineers' grey/yellow 'Dutch' with Transrail logos
CEL   Celsa black with orange cab
CEM   Cemex white and blue
CFD   Chemins de fer Départméntaux orange
CMX   Cemex white (GBRf)

COL   Colas Rail Freight orange, yellow and black
CON   Continental rail blue
COR   Corus silver
COT   BZK Cotswold Rail silver
COU   Colas Rail Freight orange, yellow and black unbranded
COY   Corus yellow
CRS   Chiltern Railways silver/grey
CSM   Continental Railway Solution maroon
DBC   DB Cargo red
DBM   DB Cargo Manager's Train silver
DBR   Deutsche Bahn all over red
DBS   DB Schenker red
DBU   DB red unbranded
DCG   Devon & Cornwall Railways green
DCN   DC Rail revised light grey
DCR   DC Rail grey
DEP   Departmental grey
DGB   BZK DRS blue with orange cab
DNS   Nederlandse Spoorwegen grey/yellow
DRA   Drax silver
DRC   DRS blue with Compass logos
DRE   DRS blue with new Compass logos (Class 88)
DRN   DRS blue with new Compass logos
DRS   blue original
DRU   DRS blue, unbranded
DRX   DRS blue with smaller Compass logos
DST   Deanside Transit lilac
EBY   Electric blue yellow panels
ECR   Euro Cargo Rail light grey
EMB   East Midlands Trains blue
EMY   GBRf with Emily Woodman graphics
EPX   Europhoenix silver
ETF   Eurovia Travaux Ferroviaires yellow
EUE   Eurostar grey with EWS logos
EUK   Eurostar grey
EWS   maroon and gold
EWR   EWS maroon and gold with RSS logos
FER   Fertis grey
FEU   Fertis grey unbranded
FGA   First Great Western blue with advertising wrap
FGB   First Great Western blue

FGO   Fragonset black unbranded
FGU   First Great Western blue unbranded
FGS   First Great Western 'special' graphics
FLG   Freightliner two tone grey
FLR   Freightliner green with yellow cabs
FLS   Freightliner green with Shanks advertising
FLY   Floyd black
FPG   Freightliner green unbranded
FPH   Freightliner 'Powerhaul' green, yellow and grey
FRG   Fragonset black
FSR   First ScotRail blue
FTF   Fall the Fallen graphics
GBB   GB Railfreight blue with orange numbers
GBF   GB Railfreight blue and orange
GBP   GB Railfreight with pride rainbows
GBR   GB Railfreight blue and orange Europorte style
GBO   GB Railfreight blue and orange original style
GBZ   GB Railfreight blue and orange with minor variations
GCR   Grand Central black
GFY   British Railways green full yellow ends
GLA   Glaxo chemicals blue and dark grey
GOP   Golden Ochre with yellow panels
GNY   British Railways green no yellow ends
GRE   Unspecified plain green
GWD   Genesee & Wyoming darker orange and black
GWO   Genesee & Wyoming lighter orange and black
GWS   British Rail green with wasp stripes
GWT   Great Western Trains all over green
GWR   Great Western Railway green
GYP   British Railways green with yellow panels
HAN   Hanson aggregates blue and silver
HAR   'Harry Patch' black graphics
HEO   Hunslet Engine Company orange/blue
HNO   Harry Needle Railroad Company orange
HOP   Hope Construction white with purple solebar
HST   Original blue, grey, yellow HST
HUN   Hunslet green
ICM   BR InterCity 'Mainline'

ICO   BR InterCity original style
ICS   BR InterCity Swallow style
IGX   BR InterCity Gatwick Express
IOS   BR InterCity original with ScotRail branding
IND   Industrial livery
JUB   DB Cargo Diamond Jubilee silver
JFU   Jarvis Fastline unbranded grey
KBR   Knorr Bremse green, white and blue
KER   Kernow black
LAB   'Laira' blue with grey roof
LAM   Lamco orange
LHO   Loadhaul original
LNE   Virgin Red with LNER branding
LNR   BZK LNWR blackberry black
LNW   LNWR grey
LON   London Midland black and green
LOR   Loram advertising graphics
LSW   LSWR black
LUB   GBRf London Transport Museum black with graphics
LUW   GBRf London Transport Museum white with graphics
MAA   DB Cargo with WH Malcolm graphics
MAL   WH Malcolm, green, yellow and blue
MAR   Lakeside & Haverthwaite Railway lined maroon
MEW   Mainline Freight blue with EWS logos
MFY   Maroon with full yellow ends
MID   Midland Railway maroon
MLB   Mainline Freight blue
MRD   DB Cargo Maritime blue
MRM   Metropolitan Railway maroon
MRT   GBRf Maritime blue
MSC   GBRf with Medite Sorrento graphics
MWS   Maroon with wasp stripes
MYP   Maroon with yellow panels
NBU   Northern Belle umber and cream unbranded
NCB   National Coal Board blue
NOB   Northern Belle umber and cream
NOR   Northern purple
NRA   National Railway Museum advertising wrap
NRB   National Railway Museum light blue
NRM   National Railway Museum maroon
NRY   Network Rail yellow

NSD	Network SouthEast revised darker blue	SCR	ScotRail Saltire blue
NSE	BZK Network SouthEast red white and blue	SCT	ScotRail HST
		SIL	Silverlink green, purple and white
NSO	Network SouthEast original with white window frames	SOU	Southern green and white
		SPE	Bombardier special purple, green, blue and red
NSR	Network SouthEast revised with blue window frames	STO	Stobart Rail advertising
ONE	Ocean Network Express magenta	SWU	South West Trains blue unbranded
OXB	Oxford blue	TAB	Tata Blue
PDP	PD Ports blue	TAS	Tata Silver
POW	Powder blue	TEW	Trainload grey with EWS logos
PUL	Pullman umber and cream	TFW	Transport for wales white and red
RCA	Railcare red white and blue	TLA	Trainload grey with Aggregates logos
RCG	Railcare grey and white	TLC	Trainload grey with Coal logos
RED	Unspecified plain red	TLH	Trainload grey with Loadhaul logos
REG	Regional Railways blue and grey	TLM	Trainload grey with Metals logos
RES	Rail Express systems red and dark grey	TMF	Trainload grey with Mainline Freight logo
REW	Railfreight Distribution 'European' two tone grey with EWS logos	TMT	Transmart Trains green
		TTG	Two tone unbranded Railfreight grey
RFD	Railfreight Distribution two tone grey with RfD logos	TRN	Transrail grey
		TSO	TSO yellow
RFE	Railfreight Distribution 'European' two tone grey with RfD logos	UKR	UK Rail Leasing grey with yellow cabs
		UND	Undercoat/unpainted/primer
RFO	Railfreight Original grey	VEA	Virgin Trains red with advertising branding
RFS	RFS grey		
RMB	RMS Locotec black	VEC	Virgin Trains East Coast With LNER Branding
RMS	RMS Locotec blue		
ROG	Rail Operations Group blue	VFS	Virgin Trains Flying Scotsman
ROY	Royal Scotsman plum	VIR	Virgin Trains red
RRB	Rush Rail Black (GBRf)	WCR	West Coast Railways maroon with yellow panels
RSR	Railfreight Red stripe		
RTC	Railway Technical Centre red and blue	XCT	CrossCountry Trains
RTO	Royal Train plum		
RTP	Royal Train Res style		

Pool codes

ATLO	Alstom Traincare Locomotives
ATZZ	Alstom Traincare Locomotives For Disposal
AWCA	West Coast Railway Operational Diesel Locomotives
AWCX	West Coast Railway Stored Diesel Locomotives
BREL	Boden Rail Engineering
CDJD	Central Services/Serco Railtest Ex Serco Shunters
CFOL	Class 50 Operations Ltd
CFSL	Class 40 Stored Locos
COFS	Colas Rail Freight
COLO	Colas Rail Freight Hire Locomotives
COLS	Colas Rail Freight Stored Locomotives
COTS	Colas Rail Freight Locomotives For Refurbishing
DBLX	Deltic Preservation Society
DDIN	Freightliner Shunter Fleet
DFGH	Freightliner Heavy Haul
DFGI	Freightliner Intermodal
DFHG	Freightliner Heavy Haul
DFHH	Freightliner Heavy Haul
DFHJ	Freightliner Heavy Haul RHTT/Limited Use
DFIM	Freightliner Intermodal Modified
DFIN	Freightliner Intermodal Low Emission
DFLC	Freightliner Intermodal
DFLH	Freightliner Heavy Haul
DFNC	Freightliner Awaiting Maintenance
DHLT	Freightliner Stored/Not In Main Line Use Locomotives
EFOO	First Great Western FGW Class 57/6
EFPC	First Great Western FGW Class 43
EFSH	First Great Western FGW Shunters
EHPC	Arriva CrossCountry HST Power Cars
EJLO	London Midland Shunters
ELRD	East Lancashire Railway Operational Locomotives
EMPC	East Midlands Trains HST Power Cars
EMSL	East Midlands Trains Shunters
EPEX	Europhoenix For Scrap/Export
EPUK	Europhoenix UK Locomotives
GBBR	GBRf Class 73/9 – Brush Repowered
GBBT	GBRf UK Cab – Long Range Fuel Tanks
GBCH	GBRf Caledonian Sleeper

GBCS	GBRf Re-Engineered
GBEB	GBRf Euro Cab – Long Range Fuel Tanks
GBED	GBRf Electro Diesel Locos For Hire
GBEE	GBRf On Hire Class 20
GBEL	GBRf Euro Cab – Standard Fuel Tanks
GBET	GBRf Stored Locos
GBFM	GBRf RETB Fitted Locomotives
GBGD	GBRf Class 56 operational
GBGS	GBRf Class 56 stored
GBHN	GBRf Long Term Hire Locomotives
GBLT	GBRf UK Cab – Standard Fuel Tanks
GBNB	GBRf New Build Locos
GBNR	GBRf For Network Rail Use
GBRT	GBRf Restricted Locos
GBSD	GBRf Stored Locos
GBSL	GBRf Caledonian Sleepers
GBST	GBRf Caledonian Sleepers/Channel Tunnel
GBWM	GBRf Shunting Duties
GBYH	GBRf General Pool
GCHP	Grand Central HST Power Cars
GPSS	Eurostar UK Operate From TI (DBC Maintained)
GROG	Rail Operations Group Operational Locos
HAPC	ScotRail Class 43
HBSH	Virgin Trains East Coast On Hire To VTEC
HISE	Rail Vehicle Engineering East Midlands Trains Shunters
HTLX	Hanson Traction Operational Locomotives
HYWD	South West Trains Thunderbird Locos
IANA	Greater Anglia Loco Fleet
IECA	Virgin Trains East Coast Operational Locomotives
IECP	Virgin Trains East Coast HST power cars
KDSD	Bombardier Doncaster
LSLO	Locomotive Services Limited, operational locos
LSLS	Locomotive Services Limited, stored locos
MBDL	Non TOC Private Owner – Diesel locos
MBED	Non TOC Private Owner – Class 73

MBEL	Non TOC Private Owner – Electric locos
MOLO	RT Rail Limited Hired Fleet Shunter locos
MRLO	RMS Locotec Ex-FM Rail Operational Locos
MRLS	RMS Locotec Ex-FM Rail Stored locos
MRSO	RMS Locotec Ex-FM Rail Operational Shunters
NRLO	Nemesis Rail Locomotives On Hire
NRLS	Nemesis Rail Ex-FM Rail Stored locos
QACL	Network Rail Load Bank
QADD	Network Rail Diesel Locos
QCAR	Network Rail HST Power Cars
QETS	Network Rail European Signalling
RCZH	Knorr Bremse Rail Systems Springburn Works Shunters
RCZN	Knorr Bremse Rail Systems Wolverton Works Shunters
RFSH	Wabtec Rail Locomotives
RMSX	RMS Locotec Locomotives
RTSO	Riviera Trains Operational Shunters
RVLO	Railway Vehicle Engineering Derby Operational Locomotives
SAXL	Eversholt Rail Off Lease Locos
SBXL	Porterbrook Leasing Off Lease Locos
SCEL	Angel Train Contracts Off Lease Locos
TTLS	Traditional Traction/Railway Support Services
UKRL	UK Rail Leasing On Lease
UMRM	UK Rail Leasing Not Main Line
UKRS	UK Rail Leasing Stored
WAAC	DB Cargo UK
WABC	DB Cargo UK RETB Fitted
WAWC	DB Cargo UK Arriva Wales Hire
WBAE	DB Cargo UK Fitted With Stop/Start Technology
WBAR	DB Cargo UK Remote Condition Monitoring Equipment
WBAT	DB Cargo UK General
WBBE	DB Cargo UK RETB & Stop/Start Technology Fitted

WBBT	DB Cargo UK RETB Fitted
WBLE	DB Cargo UK Lickey Bankers With Stop/Start Technology
WBLT	DB Cargo UK
WBTT	DB Cargo UK RHTT – Tripcock Fitted
WCAT	DB Cargo UK Standard Fuel Range
WCBT	DB Cargo UK Extended Fuel Rail
WDAM	DB Cargo UK
WEAC	DB Cargo UK
WFBC	DB Cargo UK HS1 Equipped
WGEA	DB Cargo UK Euro Cargo Rail
WGEE	DB Cargo UK Eastern Europe
WGEP	DB Cargo UK Poland
WQAA	DB Cargo UK Locomotives Stopped Serviceable – Group 1A
WQAB	DB Cargo UK Stored Locomotives Group 1B
WQBA	DB Cargo UK Stored Locomotives Stored Serviceable – Group 2
WQCA	DB Cargo UK Stored Locos For Component Recovery – Group 3
WQDA	DB Cargo UK Stored Locomotives Surplus - Group 4
XHAC	Direct Rail Services Operational Locos – ETS Equipped
XHCC	Direct Rail Services Operational Locos – Northern (Cumbrian Coast Workings)
XHCE	Direct Rail Services Hire To Chiltern Railways
XHCK	Direct Rail Services Operational Locos
XHIM	Direct Rail Services Intermodal Locos
XHNC	Direct Rail Services Nuclear Traffic
XHSS	Direct Rail Services Stored Locos
XHTP	Direct Rail Services Locos For Transpennine Express
XHVE	Direct Rail Services Vossloh Locos
XHVT	Direct Rail Services West Coast Thunderbird Locos
XYPA	Mendip Rail Operational Locomotives
XYPO	Mendip Rail Operational Locomotives

Depot codes

AB	Albacete, Spain Continental Rail		CF	Cardiff Canton Colas Rail Freight
AC	Alicante, Spain Transfesa		CL	Crewe LNWR
AH	Asfordby Technical Centre Network Rail		CM	Cambridge Arriva CrossCountry
AN	Allerton Alstom		CO	Coquelles, France Eurotunnel
AR	Attero Recycling Doncaster		CQ	Crewe Railway Age Trust
AT	Attercliffe European Metal Recycling		CP	Crewe Carriage Shed Arriva
AZ	Alizay, Nr. Rouen, France DB Cargo		CR	Crewe Gresty Bridge Direct Rail Services
BB	Billingham Sembcorp Utilities		CS	Carnforth West Coast Railways
BD	Boston Docks Victoria Group		CZ	Burton Central Rivers Bombardier
BH	Barrow Hill Roundhouse		DC	Craiova Romania exported locos DB Cargo
BK	Bristol Barton Hill LNWR		DD	Daventry International Railfreight Terminal
BL	Loughborough Falcon Works Wabtec/Bruch Traction			Malcolm Rail
BM	Bournemouth West South Western Railway		DF	Derby RTC Loram (UK)
BN	Bounds Green Virgin Trains East Coast		DG	Dagenham
BO	Bo'ness Scottish Railway Preservation Society		DK	Konkar Bulgaria exported locos DB Cargo
BQ	Bury East Lancs Railway		DL	Dean Lane Manchester
BS	Bescot DB Cargo		DM	Dollands Moor Eurotunnel
BU	Burton upon Trent Nemesis Rail		DS	Deanside Transit
BZ	Sofia, Bulgaria BZK Българска Жеиезолътна Компания		DY	Derby Etches Park East Midlands Trains
CA	Castle Donington storage site		EC	Craigentinny Virgin Trains East Coast
CB	Crewe Basford Hall Network Rail		EG	Liverpool Edge Hill Alstom
CC	Cardiff Steelworks Celsa		EK	Shepherdswell East Kent Railway
CD	Crewe DMD Locomotive Services Limited		EH	Eastleigh DB Cargo
CE	Crewe International Electric DB Cargo		EY	Ely Potter Group Logistics
			FD	Mobile Maintenance, Mainline Diesels Freightliner

FE	Mobile Maintenance, Mainline Electrics Freightliner
FG	Garston Ford
FP	Mobile Maintenance, Poland Freightliner
FS	Mobile Maintenance, Diesel Shunters Freightliner
FT	Fréthun, France DB Cargo
FX	Felixstowe Freightliner
GO	Grosmont North Yorkshire Moors Railway
HA	Haymarket ScotRail
HH	Hams Hall Associated British Ports
HO	Hope Hope Construction
HQ	Headquarters
HT	Newcastle Heaton Northern/Grand Central
HUN	Hungary Floyd
IN	UK Industrial Sites
IS	Inverness ScotRail
KM	Carlisle Kingmoor Direct Rail Services
KR	Kidderminster Severn Valley Railway
KT	Ketton Cement Works Heidelburg Cement Group
KY	Knottingley DB Cargo
LA	Plymouth Laira Great Western Railway
LD	Leeds Midland Road Freightliner
LE	Swansea Landore Great Western Railway
LG	Manchester Longsight Electric Alstom
LH	Barton-under-Needwood LH Group Services (Wabtec)
LM	Long Marston Quiton Rail

LO	Manchester Longsight Diesel Alstom
LR	Leicester UK Rail Leasing
LW	Longtown (Smalmstown) MoD
MA	Manchester International Traincare Alstom
MB	Middlesbrough AV Dawson
MD	Merehead Aggregated Industries
MG	Margam DB Cargo
MQ	Machen Quarry Hanson Aggregates
MR	Margate Locomotive Services Limited
NC	Norwich Crown Point Abellio Greater Anglia
NE	Nottingham Eastcroft Boden Rail
NL	Neville Hill East Midlands Trains
OO	Old Oak Common HST Great Western Railway
OY	Oxley Alstom
PD	Teesport PD Ports
PG	Peterborough GB Railfreight
PF	Peak Forest GB Railfreight
PM	Bristol St Philip's Marsh Great Western Railway
PN	Rybnik/Poznan, Poland DB Cargo
PO	Polmadie Alstom
PU	Immingham Puma Energy
PZ	Penzance Great Western Railway
RR	Doncaster Roberts Road EMD/GB Railfreight
RU	Rugby Rail Plant Colas Rail Freight
SB	Shrewsbury Coleham Yard Network Rail

SC	Scunthorpe Steelworks Tata Steel
SE	St Leonards St Leonards Engineering
SH	Southall Railway Centre West Coast Railways
SI	Soho London Midland
SK	Swanwick Midland Railway Butterley
SL	Stewarts Lane Southern
SM	Southampton Maritime Freightliner
SO	Southall WCR/LSL
SP	Wigan Springs Branch DB Cargo
SS	Shotton Steelworks Tata Steel
TC	Toton Training Compound DB Cargo
TI	Temple Mills International Eurostar
TM	Tyseley Locomotive Works Vintage Trains
TO	Toton DB Cargo
TR	Trostre Steelworks Tata Steel
TS	Tyseley London Midland
TX	Thuxton Mid Norfolk Railway
TY	Toton Yard DB Cargo
WB	Wembley Traincare Alstom
WC	Washwood Heath Cemex
WD	Widnes Alstom
WG	Whitemoor Yard GB Railfreight
WH	Washwood Heath Boden Rail Engineering/DC Rail
WI	Wishaw Moveright International
WK	Worksop

WN	Willesden GBRf/LOROL
WO	Wolsingham Weardale Railway
WP	Woippy, France DB Cargo
WQ	Headquarters
WR	Leeming Bar Wensleydale Railway
WY	Westbury Yard DB Cargo
WZ	Warsaw, Poland Freightliner
YK	York National Railway Museum
ZA	Derby RTC Business Park Loram
ZB	Doncaster Works Wabtec
ZC	Crewe Works, Bombardier Transportation
ZD	Derby Litchurch Lane Works Bombardier Transportation
ZG	Eastleigh Works Arlington Fleet Group
ZH	Glasgow Springburn, Works Knorr Bremse Rail Systems
ZI	Ilford Level 5 Works Bombardier Transportation
ZK	Kilmarnock Works Wabtec
ZN	Wolverton Works Knorr Bremse Rail Systems
ZO	Kingsbury European Metal Recycling
ZR	Rotherham CF Booth Ltd
ZS	Wakefield RMS Locotec
ZW	Stoke On Trent Works Axiom Rail/Turners/Marcroft
ZZ	loco yet to arrive in the UK GB Railfreight

Owner codes

ACL	AC Locomotive Group	FLI	Freightliner
AGI	Aggregates Industries	GAR	Garcia Hanson
AGO	Andrew Goodman	GBR	GB Railfreight
ALS	Alstom	GWR	Great Western Railway
ANG	Angel Trains	HAN	Hanson Aggregates
ARV	Arriva Group	HJE	Howard Johnston
BEA	Beacon Rail	HNR	Harry Needle Railroad Company
BEV	Beaver Sports	LES	Les Ross
BEN	Steve Beniston	LOL	London Overground
BOD	Neil Boden	LOM	Lombard Finance
CAP	Cappagh Group (DC Rail)	LON	London Midland
CFA	Class 50 Alliance	LSL	Locomotive Services Limited
CFP	Class 40 Preservation Society	MAQ	Macquarie Group
CFS	Class 56 Group	MOW	Michael Owen
COL	Colas Rail Freight	NEM	Nemesis Rail
CTL	Class 20 Locomotive Society	NET	Network Rail
DBC	DB Cargo	NRM	National Railway Museum
DCR	DC Rail	POR	Porterbrook
DPS	Deltic Preservation Society	ROG	Rail Operations Group
DRS	Direct Rail Services	SFG	Stratford Class 47 Group
DTG	Diesel Traction Group	SOA	71A Locomotives
EEG	English Electric Group	SRP	Scottish Railway Preservation Society
EMT	East Midlands Trains	STG	Scottish Class 37 Group
EPX	Europhoenix	UKR	UK Rail Leasing
EUK	Eurostar	VIN	Vintage Trains
EVS	Eversholt Leasing	WCR	West Coast Railways
FIR	First Group		

Spot hire/industrial owners

AFS	Arlington Fleet Services	KBR	Knorr Bremse
AVD	AV Dawson	LAM	Lamco Mining
BOM	Bombardier	LOR	Loram
BMT	Bulmarket (Bulgaria)	NYM	North Yorkshire Moors Railway
BZK	BZK (Българска Жеиезолътна Компания – Bulgaria)	RFL	Reid Freight Longtown
		RSS	Railway Support Services (Traditional Traction)
CON	Continental Rail Solutions (Hungary)		
CRB	Chris Beet	SEC	Serco
EMD	Electromotive Diesels	SLE	St Leonards Engineering
EMR	European Metal Recycling	TFA	Transfesa
FLY	Floyd (Hungary)	TMT	Transmart Trains
HUN	Hunslet Engine Company	TLW	Tyseley Locomotive Works
ITY	Private owner in Italy	VIC	Victoria Group (Boston Docks)

Heritage railway locations

WAB — Wabtec
ALL — Allely's yard, Studley
ALN — Aln Valley Railway
AVR — Avon Valley Railway
BAT — Battlefield Line
BH — Barrow Hill Roundhouse
BKR — Bo'ness & Kinneil Railway
BIR — Barry Island Railway
BLU — Bluebell Railway
BRC — Buckingham Railway Centre
BWR — Bodmin & Wenford Railway
BU — Burton on Trent
CAL — Caledonian Railway
CHR — Chasewater Railway
CHV — Churnet Valley Railway
CPR — Chinnor & Princes Risborough Railway
CRT — Cambrian Railways Trust
CWR — Cholsey & Wallingford Railway
CVR — Colne Valley Railway
DFR — Dean Forest Railway
DAR — Dartmoor Railway
DRC — Didcot Railway Centre
DVR — Derwent Valley Light Railway
EBR — Embsay Steam Railway
EDR — Eden Valley Railway
EKR — East Kent Railway
ELR — East Lancashire Railway

EOR — Epping and Ongar Railway
ESR — East Somerset Railway
EVR — Ecclesbourne Valley Railway
FHR — Fawley Hill Railway
GWR — Gloucestershire Warwickshire Railway
GCR — Great Central Railway
GCN — Great Central Railway Nottingham
GIR — Gwili Railway
IWR — Isle of Wight Steam Railway
KWV — Keighley & Worth Valley Railway
KES — Kent & East Sussex Railway
LHR — Lakeside & Haverthwaite Railway
LLR — Llangollen Railway
LWR — Lincolnshire Wolds Railway
MAL — Private site Malton
MHR — Mid Hants Railway
MNR — Mid Norfolk Railway
MOL — Moreton-on-Lugg
MRB — Midland Railway – Butterley
MRM — Mangapps Railway Museum
NRM — National Railway Museum York
NRS — National Railway Museum Shildon
NLR — Northampton and Lamport Railway
NNR — North Norfolk Railway

NVR — Nene Valley Railway
NYM — North Yorkshire Moors Railway
NTR — North Tyneside Railway
PBR — Pontypool & Blaenavon Railway
PDR — Paignton & Dartmouth Railway
PKR — Peak Rail
PVR — Plym Valley Railway
RAC — Railway Age Crewe
RDR — Royal Deeside Railway
RFL — Reid Freight, Longton
RHR — Rushden Heritage Railway
RSR — Ribble Steam Railway
RVR — Rother Valley Railway
SCR — Swindon & Cricklade Railway
SDR — South Devon Railway
SPA — Spa Valley Railway
STM — Stainmoor Railway
STR — Strathspey Railway
SWR — Swanage Railway
SVR — Severn Valley Railway
TBR — Trawsfynydd & Blaenau Railway
TIT — Titley Junction
TSR — Telford Steam Railway
VBR — Vale of Berkeley Railway
WH — Washwood Heath
WI — Wishaw
WEN — Weardale Railway
WEA — Wensleydale Railway
WSR — West Somerset Railway